Grandfather's Search
for
Grandson

JIM KUTY

Inspiring Voices®
A Service of **Guideposts**

Inspiring Voices books may be ordered through booksellers or by contacting:

Inspiring Voices
1663 Liberty Drive
Bloomington, IN 47403
www.inspiringvoices.com
1-(866) 697-5313

ISBN: 978-1-4624-0622-7 (sc)
ISBN: 978-1-4624-0623-4 (e)

Library of Congress Control Number: 2013908758

Printed in the United States of America.

Inspiring Voices rev. date: 06/11/2013

Table of Contents

This book is dedicated to James Robert Freels III.
WHO ELSE!

Special Thanks To

Margaret Haner—Maureen's mother. She supplied the letters which led us to Guatemala.

Bill Cregar—a retired FBI director, who working for Du Pont, became one of my advisors.

Leo Crampsey—also a retired FBI agent, who worked for Bill Cregar and was a former Regional Security Officer in the U.S. Embassy in Guatemala. Without Leo, his daily consultation, contacts in the Central Americans Embassies, and wisdom, the rescue would never have happened.

Jorge Lemus—a Guatemala U.S. Embassy worker, who determined that Bob, Maureen and Jimmy were in Guatemala and without the permission of the embassy, worked undercover for me.

Susan Rodgers—a stranger and travel agent I met by chance on the airplane to Guatemala. She led me to her influential brother, Andy Rodgers.

Andy Rodgers—Susan Rodgers brother, who orchestrated the recovery in Guatemala.

Maria Louisa Beltranena—the lawyer who handled the legal work and assisted me in Guatemala.

Cecil Nelson—owner of Cecil Nelson Detective Agency was always there when I needed him.

Inspiring Voices—a division of Guidepost Magazine. Their patience and guidance permitted me to publish this book.

To the many people that helped and who encouraged me when I was discouraged and down—and—out.

And to my beloved family who made my hardships tolerable.

Preface

My youngest of two daughters, Deborah Ann Kuty (Debbie), met James Robert Freels Jr, (Bob), at a party in Philadelphia, Pennsylvania, in 1972. Debbie was attending the Franklin Dental School in Philadelphia and Bob was a marine stationed in Lakehurst Air Station, (the site of the Hindenburg tragedy), in New Jersey. They established a relationship, on February 17, 1973 they were married. Shortly thereafter, Bob was transferred to Camp Legeune and they took up residence in Jackson, North Carolina. Their daughter, Dawn, was born there in September of 1973. Bob was then shipped overseas to Japan for a year. Debbie came to live with us during that time. Upon his return, he was assigned to the marine base in Quantico, Virginia. From there he was discharged. He tried to re-enlist, but he had an altercation with a marine officer and they wouldn't re-enlist him.

Debbie, Bob, and Dawn moved to Murfreesboro, Tennessee, near Bob's parents in 1974. It was there, in 1977 Jimmy, (the subject of this story), was born.

It was in 1977 when Debbie left Bob and moved back to New Jersey. I bought a house for her, one half mile from my wife, Mary Ann and me, in Woodstown, New Jersey.

Unfortunately, Debbie allowed Bob to move back in with her. This lasted until 1984 when they separated again. At which time Debbie filed for divorce. She was awarded custody of both children and Bob received visitation rights once every two weeks.

Bob abducted Jimmy in June of 1985.

CHAPTER 1

Day one—The Abduction

My wife and I were in bed watching TV when the phone rang around 10:00pm. It was our daughter, Debbie. She was hysterical.

"They've taken Jimmy. I just know it!" she screamed over the phone.

"Hold on! Calm down. Who's taken Jimmy? What are you talking about?"

Jimmy was my eight year old grandson. His father, James Robert Freels Jr, (Bob or Jim), who had been separated from my daughter for about a year, picked up Jimmy on the last day of school for the year, June 21, 1985.

Bob had made arrangements with Debbie to take Jimmy on a one week vacation, with his girlfriend, Maureen Wilkin, to her mother, Margaret Haner's home in Wellsboro, Pennsylvania. They were due back Sunday, June 30th.

"Bob told me they'd have Jimmy back by eight o'clock. They're two hours late." Debbie was sobbing. "I know they took him somewhere. Oh Dad, what'll we do?"

"Come on over, let's talk," I said. Debbie only lives a half mile away.

I told Mary Ann about the phone conversation. "I can't figure why she's so upset," I said, sitting on the edge of the bed. "For God's sake, the boy's only two hours late. They could be stuck in traffic or have a flat tire."

"Maybe they decided to stay another day, but they should have called Debbie," Mary Ann said.

Later I learned, Debbie had several clues that something might happen. For instance, Bob broke into Debbie's basement taking more clothes for Jimmy than she had packed for a one week vacation. A neighbor, Mel Lewis, saw him kick in the basement door. Also, he was driving a new Volvo and on a recent visit he was sporting diamond rings. His explanation to Debbie was his girlfriend inherited some money and purchased these items.

We live in Woodstown, New Jersey, where a goodly number of the 3,500 residents live in houses that go back 300 years. Not our house. I built our house in 1956-1957 at the age of twenty four. Woodstown is situated in Salem County, one of the few "garden" spots left in the Garden State.

As I was leaving the bedroom, I saw headlights coming in the driveway. It was Debbie. Before leaving home, she had awakened her daughter, Dawn, and told her to call if Jimmy came home. Dawn was twelve years old.

Debbie is normally even tempered and doesn't get riled easily. She takes after me. But she was a different Debbie who walked into the house that night. She was crying and talking at the same time. Mostly she repeated what she had said on the phone. She was absolutely convinced that Jimmy had been abducted, only she used the word kidnapped.

Mary Ann and I thought Debbie was jumping to conclusions, at least maybe that's what we wanted to think.

Bob was a former marine from Tennessee, a real macho type. Debbie had married him in 1973. He and I had never hit it off, but I had no reason to think he'd run away with his son. Who would do something like that?

"Let's wait until midnight," I cautioned. "If we don't hear anything by then, we'll go to the State Police."

We were relieved when the clock struck midnight. Not because anyone felt better, but because the kind of tension that builds up and finally would be broken by doing something.

"We can't do anything until tomorrow," said the desk sergeant at the State Police barracks. I said, "Today is our tomorrow," this didn't help. The State Police barracks is one mile outside Woodstown, on route 40, across from Cowtown, New Jersey, the only professional rodeo east of the Mississippi.

We waited an hour and a half for that!!

This started a useless chain of events dealing with law enforcement.

Back at my house, we sat around the kitchen table and talked until three o'clock in the morning. Talks around kitchen tables often have been very productive, especially ours. Decisions great and small have been made there. Tears have been shed, tempers have been lost, and wisdom occasionally found.

It was during this late night talk that Debbie, who normally is very quiet, revealed some things Mary Ann and I didn't know.

"Sometimes when Bob would get mad," Debbie confessed, "He would threaten to take Jimmy some place where I would never find him." She added for good measure that he also said, "All the money your father has isn't going to help one damn bit."

Some months before, Debbie said, she discovered hidden away in a drawer, a booklet entitled, "100 Ways to Disappear and Live Free." Had he followed the material to a tee, we never would have found him.

She also, said, "Bob subscribed to the SOLDIER of FORTUNE magazine and talked often of becoming a mercenary."

"Why didn't you ever tell us about all this before?" Mary Ann and I asked in unison.

"I don't know, maybe because Bob was always sounding off about some big deal, some outlandish plan. He was going to fly to Africa and take part in some war or he was going to Central America to fight commies. I never figured he'd do any of it. But when he didn't bring Jimmy home last night, everything came together. I knew then he'd made good on his threats and taken Jimmy with him." Debbie started to cry again.

This is the way I perceived Bob, a dreamer, who never made sense to me. He was not a doer. This is why I had a hard time accepting him taking JIMMY.

The discussion broke up at three in the morning and we didn't sleep well for what little remained of the night.

CHAPTER 2

The Second Day-Trying to Sort Things Out

The next day, Monday, June, 31, 1985, I went to work as usual. I was a Process Staff Engineer in the Atomic Energy Division (AED) at Du Pont's headquarters in Wilmington, Delaware, The Atomic Energy Division managed the massive nuclear plant Du Pont built for the government in South Carolina, for the manufacture of plutonium. My office was a fifteen minute drive from my home in Woodstown, New Jersey. My efficiency at the office that day was near zero.

Debbie had scared my wife and me with her disclosures, but I was still skeptical that they had left the area.

When I got home from the office, Debbie was at my house waiting for me. I learned Debbie went to her job at a bank in Mullica Hill, New Jersey, a nearby town that morning, Her condition was not much improved from the night before. Her supervisor, Joe Doble, asked her what was wrong and she blurted out the story as she knew it then.

Her supervisor contacted the bank's attorney, George Rosenberger, who recommended hiring a detective agency, and filing an official complaint with the Woodstown Municipal Court clerk.

Her supervisor sent her home.

Debbie did file a complaint, charging Bob with taking Jimmy, for "lawful custody without permission."

During dinner, we decided to visit Bob and Maureen's apartment at 414 West Main Street in Norristown, Pennsylvania, that evening. Norristown is located north west of Philadelphia, about an hour from Woodstown. The "we" included Debbie, Debbie's boyfriend "Butch" Canzanese, Dawn, and my brother-in-law Martin Mlinek, who lives next door to me.

Twelve year old Dawn had been to the apartment several times with her brother Jimmy on regular visits. She was helpful locating the apartment.

Bob and Maureen lived on the second floor of a two story apartment building in a run-down neighborhood not far from the business district.

As we walked up the stairs, we saw a note tacked to the front door of the apartment. It was from a Norristown Police Officer, Sergeant Ricco, It was dated June 25th, and it asked, "Maureen contact your mother, she is worried about you." June 25th was Tuesday. Bob, Maureen and Jimmy were supposed to have been at her mother's then.

My heart skipped a couple beats. My God, I thought, it appears Debbie's fear was justified. It looks like we have a kidnapping.

· We also noticed that the mail carrier was still leaving mail addressed to Bob and Maureen. Their mailbox was full and some mail was stacked on the stairs. I leafed through the mail, which included a SOLDIER of FORTUNE magazine, bills, personal letters and the usual collection of catalogs.

My first instinct was to open personal letters, a telephone bill— anything that might provide a clue to the whereabouts of Bob, Maureen and Jimmy. But the small voice of conscience whispered, "Don't touch; federal offense, you know."

I banged on the apartment door a couple times. No response. We were about to leave when the door opened and a young man who identified himself as the landlord's son invited us in. He and a friend were cleaning.

The apartment consisted of a large living room and a kitchen-dining room combination. A back room evidently had been used as a den. Two bedrooms were up a short flight of stairs. The place was nearly empty.

The young man called his father, Bob Mancini, and I got on the phone. He said Bob and Maureen apparently had abandoned the apartment, although they had told him they were going to replace the furniture they had removed over a week ago with new pieces and planned to renew the rental agreement for another year.

"I don't think they're coming back," the landlord said. I said, "I think your right." "Also, their check for June rent bounced," he said.

The only things left in the apartment were a coffeemaker, air conditioner, several plants, two bowling balls and Bob and Maureen's winter clothes.

Their winter clothes! Oh Jesus, I thought, what does that mean. Without saying it out loud, I think everyone in the apartment knew what that meant. They were headed where they weren't going to need winter clothes—ever.

And they probably had over a two week head start on anyone trying to follow them. It now seemed obvious that when they picked up Jimmy on June 21 to take him to the north country for a week's vacation, they had instead turned south to God knows where.

We split up to search the place thoroughly. We must have been well coached by decades of cop shows on television because we even went through wastebaskets.

It didn't hurt then, or later, that I had once been in charge of security at Du Pont's sprawling Chamber's Works Plant in Deepwater, New Jersey. I wasn't a highly trained investigator, not by a long shot, but I had learned on the job the importance of looking carefully, asking hard questions and listening attentively.

One item among the trash gave us another jolt. It was a pilot's log which showed that Bob had been learning how to fly a helicopter.

Geez, I thought, he's become a mercenary for sure. Maybe the SOB has taken my grandson to Nicaragua! I had a fleeting vision of this little kid in his Phillies tee shirt slogging through mud and jungle as the gringo mascot for some contra patrol.

Also, in the basket was a note dated June 14th from someone named Tom, advising Bob that he had a buyer for his furniture. Learned later Tom was Tom Bleming, a friend of Bob, who was a mercenary and knew of the abduction. The date, June 14th, showed they were planning the abduction weeks, maybe months in advance.

The only other item of interest was a business card for James H. Wilkin pinned to the bulletin board. I presumed it was Maureen's ex-husband. I stuck it in my pocket. Later that day, I called him.

The five of us left the apartment and drove to the Norristown Police Department. No one said much. I think each of us was imagining some version of a scenario in which Jimmy was in the clutches of his hairbrained father and living in squalor and danger in some God-forsaken land.

Naturally, the officer who had left the note on the apartment door was off duty, but I did get his name and a telephone number.

I then called Jim Wilkin, Maureen's ex-husband. He said he had just returned from a honeymoon with his second wife a week ago and that his (and Maureen's) eleven-year old daughter, Bevin, had been trying to reach her mother, Maureen, ever since. He also gave me Maureen's mother's name, Margaret "Peg" Haner, and her phone number.

The drive back to Woodstown seemed to take double the time of the trip there. Everyone was scared, mad and confused, maybe in equal parts. But no one was anxious to voice these feelings for fear of upsetting the others, particularly Debbie, who was just barely in control of her emotions, and Dawn, who was just old enough to worry and spend the rest of her summer nights having terrible nightmares about her little brother.

CHAPTER 3

The next week

The next day I contacted and employed a Philadelphia detective agency, Waltman and Associates, which said for a $500 retainer they would try to trace Bob and Maureen through credit card expenditures on the road—if they had any. It turned out they didn't. This item was covered in their booklet "100 Ways to Disappear and Live Free."

I was intrigued with the mail that was in the apartment. I decided to go with Debbie to the Norristown Post Office and take out a PO Box as Mrs. Robert Freels (she and Bob were legally separated but not divorced yet). She asked the postmaster to put her husband's mail in her box. "Do you want the accumulated mail?" she was asked. Naturally, she said "Yes."

This move was <u>very helpful</u> in starting the investigation.

The telephones bills were very revealing. They showed Bob called all the Central American Embassies in New York shortly before leaving. He also called, John Cattle, the leader of the American Freedom Fighters (AFF), a mercenary group in Camden, Tennessee several times just before he left with Jimmy. These calls contributed immensely to the story. The AFF's charter is to fight Communist aggression. They also solicit aid for the then Nicaraguan, "contra" effort.

I made an entry in the journal I had just begun: "A very bad Fourth of July without Jimmy." The worst part was not knowing whether next year or any Independence Day, thereafter, would find Jimmy wolfing down hamburgers as fast as I flipped them off the grill.

I followed up during the week by calling Sgt. Ricco of the Norristown Police Department. He told me he was called by Maureen's mother reporting her missing and by her employer. He got permission from her mother to enter the apartment. The apartment was empty and no one was there. There was concern there may have been foul play.

Again I talked to James Wilkin. He told me Maureen sang in a choir on Wednesday nights and that Maureen's mother told him she hadn't heard from Maureen in over three weeks. He said, Maureen had told him a month or so before that she may get behind on her support payments because the new Volvo she got would tax her finances.

Most of the time that week, when I wasn't working in my office in Wilmington, I tried in vain to get Jimmy listed by the National Crime Information Center (NCIC) as a missing person who had been unlawfully abducted by his father. The NCIC is a national center that collects data from all over the states that involves police work. It records automobile tickets and anyone wanted by the police. I expended considerable effort trying to get them on the NCIC. At this time, I didn't know if they were still in the states or not. I visited the Woodstown Police Department several times during the week to try and get them put on the NCIC. I got all kinds of excuses, like it's a misdemeanor and we've turned it over to the Prosecutor's Office.

That Sunday, I went golfing in the morning. In the club house, I met a man from the prosecutor's office in neighboring Cumberland County, who, in response to my questions, said he thought Debbie could file a charge of kidnapping against Bob.

That afternoon, Mary Ann and I headed to the New Jersey shore about one hour away. My purpose was to catch up to Frank Hoerst, the Salem County Prosecutor, who I was told by his office, was spending the weekend at his place in Townsends Inlet, near Avalon. I was hoping I could get Frank, who I knew personally, to expedite getting Bob on the NCIC.

However, on the way we stopped at the house in Ocean City owned by Ham Fowser, my best friend and skiing buddy. The house fronts on the beach. Ham was lounging in a chair down by the water and we trudged through the soft white sand to reach him. He introduced us to the man sitting next to him who was still dripping wet from a plunge into the surf. The man's name was George Joo and was renting the second floor apartment in Ham's house. He was also a detective with the New Jersey State Police.

I decided Detective Joo was a captive audience. Since he had just been in the water, it was unlikely he would try to escape me by making a sudden dash for the waves. In fact, he gave every indication of settling in for an afternoon bake. I squatted in front of his chair, and told him everything that had happened since last Sunday.

To my surprise, he seemed to be absorbed by the tale and empathetic toward our fears and frustrations. But then he gave us the bad news: "abduction of a child by his parent is not a felony in New Jersey, it's a misdemeanor."

"I don't believe it! You mean Bob can kidnap my grandson and it isn't any more serious than doing 40 in a 25 mile an hour zone?"

"Well, sort of."

"What the hell is this country coming to?"

"Not the country. The problem is New Jersey. It's a felony in Pennsylvania," George Joo said.

"Hey, they took Jimmy into Pennsylvania saying they were going on vacation, so . . . ."

"Nope. Won't do. It happened in New Jersey. Sorry."

"How about that guy from the prosecutor's office in Cumberland County, he said, we could press kidnapping charges against Bob?"

"I'm pretty sure his information is incorrect." Joo was trying to be diplomatic.

"If the kidnapping is only a misdemeanor, who is going to pursue this creep and bring him to justice?" I asked. And, "If he's slipped into Mexico or some other country, what government is going to extradite him for a freakin' misdemeanor?" Here I was taking out my frustration and anger on this poor guy who was giving up his vacation time on the beach to listen to a total stranger telling his tale of woe.

I had been sitting on my haunches all this time. Now, I fell back into the sand with my hands over my eyes. They hurt from the sun.

Joo soothed my anguish. "If you want, I can make a call about the NCIC thing. We should be able to get information on the network."

I got up and together we walked back to Ham's house. Joo telephoned a colleague, Wayne Price, who worked in the Missing Persons Division of the State Police. When he hung up, he said Price would await my call tomorrow and would take all the information necessary for the NCIC.

Later, when everyone was off the beach and back in the house, I dialed the number I had for Frank Hoerst. His brother-in-law answered and said Hoerst had already left for Woodstown.

With the sun setting, we bid goodbye to Ham and Detective Joo and headed home. Mary Ann and I didn't speak until we were nearly there.

"Jim, are we ever going to see our grandson again?" Mary Ann had remained pretty calm throughout this whole lousy week. I knew she was hurting inside, but on the outside she had been the voice of hope and optimism. Now I thought I heard fear and despair.

"I don't know, hon. It sure is discouraging, isn't it?"

"What do we do? What can we do?" Mary Ann asked.

I guess I thought the NCIC alert, if we ever could get it, would help stop them, but I'm not so sure anymore. No police are going to go out of their way to arrest someone who's charged only with a misdemeanor. That's what upsets me the most. A man steals a child against his will, deceives his mother, who has legal custody, takes him across state lines, maybe a border or two, and he's no more guilty than somebody down the street who lets his dog out without a license."

"I know, I know. The system stinks, but, Jim, what—do—we—do?" She was expecting me to have a good answer. I had none.

After a week of trying to get local police to assist me and put Bob, Maureen and Jimmy on the NCIC, I cornered the Chief of Police in the Woodstown station. He told me he had assigned one of his staff to investigate. To this day, no officer has yet to interview me or my daughter. I demanded Bob be put on the NCIC. His answer was they are very busy with a recent robbery.

It was then I vowed to myself and family that the only person that was going to find my grandson was me. And I would never—never give up.

CHAPTER 4

Meeting with Maureen's Mother

Two weeks after we learned of the abduction, we made arrangements to meet with Maureen's mother. I decided that if we found Jimmy it would be through Maureen. Bob was too crafty, and had the benefit of devious advisers and the pamphlet, "100 Ways to Disappear and Live Free."

On Sunday, July 14, 1985, Debbie, Dawn and I left for Wellsboro, Pennsylvania, to meet with Margaret Pane (Peg) Haner, Maureen's mother. It was a five and a half hour drive. "Peg" was extremely cooperative and helpful. She was living with her sister, June, in a trailer park. We spoke for two and a half hours.

"Peg" was grateful someone was doing something. She was just beginning to realize her daughter left, maybe the country, without a word. Particularly upsetting was she left her eleven year old daughter, Bevin, without even a goodbye.

She told us the first time she met Bob was in April of 1985. He had driven there in a Lincoln Continental with Maureen and Jimmy, and a trunk full of guns in a duffel bag, including a machine gun. He wanted to test fire them somewhere. She sent him down the road to William Davis, who had a makeshift practice range. "Bob really scared me." "Peg" said. Also, Maureen had told her that Bob was thinking of going to South America "to make lots of money."

According to "Peg", Maureen received $14,000 from her grandfather's estate. She wired the money to a bank in May. Maureen owed "Peg" money so she reduced the amount wired to pay the debt. She said, "I'm thankful I did that."

"Peg" gave me names and phone numbers of Maureen's former and present friends. I called most of them but their knowledge was vague and most of them said they were going to South America.

One close friend whose name surfaced was Jane Leathersich. I talked with Jane several times and although she wasn't able to contribute much, she was interested in what was happening. She called throughout the following months.

Maureen's pastor, Lamont Satterly, a good friend, advisor and a Sunday school teacher was more talkative. He knew Jim Wilkin, her ex-husband also. He said, "He could understand how Maureen's adventurous spirit could be enticed by someone like Bob. However, her strong family ties and roots will cause her to return to Wellsboro."

"Peg" told us, "Tony Maddonia was Maureen's boyfriend before she met Bob." She gave his address in Norristown and phone number.

The following weekend MaryAnn and I went to visit him in Norristown, Pennsylvania. Tony owned a music store and above the store was an apartment.

We introduced ourselves. Tony initially was very reserved. I guess he was wondering who we were and what our purpose was. We shared our story and when we mentioned Maureen's mother told us she just inherited $14,000, his jaw dropped. "Oh my God," he nearly shouted. "I loaned her $14,000. It looks like I'll never get it back." He then became talkative and relayed his association with Maureen.

This is what Tony told us.

He met Maureen at a church gathering in April of 1984. They became very close. He offered her his apartment rent free. He was a widower, his wife died in childbirth four years before. He had two boys, one fifteen the other four years old. He was lonely and vulnerable and thought she "answered his prayers." They got into a deep relationship. Marriage was discussed. He met her mother and she his. He loaned her $14,000. She never returned it.

One night in July of 1984, around midnight he was outside, it was hot and he couldn't sleep. Maureen's lights were on in her second floor apartment. At 4:00am a man wearing a security uniform came out. The man, believed to be Bob, got in a car and drove around the block and came back. When he did, Maureen came down, handed him something and he left. Tony was crushed. After a few days he ordered her out because he was devastated.

After not seeing or hearing from her for nearly nine months, in March of 1985, he received a letter from her. It had no return address. She indicated she was desperate; her only alternative was bankruptcy or suicide. She mentioned she may come into money. Tony had no idea why she sent him that letter.

After our visit with Tony, he realized Maureen was gone and so was his $14,000.

In the weeks and months that followed I was very busy. I spent too much time hounding the local police. It was suggested that a "Trap" be put on my daughter's telephone in case she got a call from Bob, so the call could be traced. The telephone company would only do this with permission from law enforcement. I contacted the Woodstown Chief of Police, Walt Simpkins. For weeks we sparred, argued and confronted one another. To no avail, it never happened.

I wrote letters to my congressmen, senators and others. Came to the conclusion there was nothing they could or would do.

To cover the possibility of them still being in the states, I printed "Missing Child" posters. Since Jimmy is with them, they probably would enroll him in school. Therefore, I got a list of every southern state school district and mailed them a copy of the poster. Obviously it didn't succeed because later we found out they were out of the country.

Poster sent to Southern School Districts

MISSING CHILD
<u>HAVE YOU SEEN THIS CHILD?</u>

NCIC: 1245 FILE 6

NAME: James Robert Freels, III (Jimmy)
DATE OF BIRTH: 3/14/1977 (8 yrs)
HEIGHT: 4' 2"　　WEIGHT: 65 lbs
HAIR: Brown, slightly wavy　EYES: Brown
MISC:
    1/2" Scar under chin
    Has freckles on nose and cheeks
    Space between upper front teeth

HOBBIES:
    Fishing, Little league baseball—
    (Played with "Hitchners" spring 1985)
    Can snow ski and bowl
    Loves riding 20" BMX bicycle
    Has collection of matchbox cars

BACKGROUND:
    Mother: Deborah Freels
        38 Hunt st.
        Woodstown, N.J.

    Sister: Dawn (12 years old)

    Schooling: Completed 1ST grade at Mary
        Shoemaker School, Woodstown, N. J.
        Teacher: Mrs. Ridgeway

    Grandparents: Jim and Mary Ann Kuty

    Friends: Brian Flitcraft and Michael Miller

Abducted by father, James R. Freels, Jr. and girlfriend, Maureen (nee Haner) Wilkin, June 21,1985 from Woodstown, N. J. Mother had legal custody. Father has been indicted and is wanted for arrest in New Jersey, Warrant: WL 97548. County of Salem in N. J. will extradite. He is Vietnam vet and worked in security. Girlfriend, Maureen, may be posing as Jimmy's mother. She is a college graduate, very versatile and may attempt to get a teaching position. They may have changed their identity. Were driving a 1985 gray Volvo, Pa. Lisc. KPU741.

IF SEEN PLEASE NOTIFY: Woodstown, N. J. Police Chief Walter Simpkins,

    609—769—2121, or your local or State Police.

CHAPTER 5

Bill Cregar—and the FBI

As I mentioned earlier, I worked for Du Pont in their Atomic Energy Division (AED), at their headquarters in Wilmington, Delaware. Employed in Du Pont's legal department was Bill Cregar. I made an appointment for July 9, 1985 to see him for advice. He was located in the same building where I worked. Bill was a retired FBI director and was formally an assistant to J. Edgar Hoover, the one time Chief of the FBI.

I told him my story. He was very attentive and asked many questions. Then he said to me, "Let me tell you my story."

Several years ago, I had a son who just finished law school. We were living in Washington, D.C. My son was twenty two years old and was on his way to a party on his behalf to celebrate his graduation. He was driving alone and stopped for a red light in downtown DC. A stranger walked up to the car and with a gun in his hand shot him in the head and killed him. An attempted robbery gone wrong.

Bill said to me, "My wife is still in a state of depression. I know how your daughter must feel not having her son. I will do anything I can to help you." He said he would get in touch with the FBI in Jackson, Tennessee and would work closely with Salem Prosecutor, Frank Hoerst, to get a warrant of arrest for Bob, in case he is picked up in the states.

Bill Cregar and I became good friends. I met with him frequently. He was a stout man, in his late fifties, muscular and still had the physique of his professional football (Steeler) days. He had a ready smile, etched in his round face and balding head. He carried himself like a soldier.

That afternoon Bill contacted the FBI in Jackson, Tennessee, and made arrangements for me to talk with, Jerry Baston, the Regional Security Officer (RSO). Jerry wanted information on Bob, Maureen and Jimmy to distribute throughout that area in case they returned to Tennessee, which I provided. He also gave me the name of a recently retired FBI agent, Joe Rasberry, who he thought could do some undercover work to find out what the America Freedom Fighters (AFF) in Camden, Tennessee might know.

I hired him for $500. Joe Rasberry reported that he talked briefly to John Cattle, the AAF head man. John is the person Bob called a couple times the day before he abducted Jimmy. John said he thought he was in Central America. Joe Rasberry then talked with a mercenary who was knowledgeable of the AFF activities. The mercenary lived in a shack "back in the hills." The place was guarded by Doberman dogs. "They tore up my cloths and scratched the hell out of me," he said, "If I'd brought my gun, I'd have shot the bastards." When I asked him if he learned anything, his response was a set back. The guy said he didn't think Freels had gone to Central America.

For God's sake, where the hell are they? Is this mercenary just trying to throw us off their trail?

When I was talking to Jerry Baston he said, "The FBI in Philadelphia are interested in Freels," He gave me Philadelphia FBI's agent, Tom Webber's phone number.

I made arrangements to meet with Tom Webber on July 17, 1985 at his office in the Federal Building in downtown Philadelphia, Pennsylvania.

After a short introduction, he surprised me with his first question, "What was my impression of Bob Freels?" I told him I didn't hold him in high regard because he's lazy, a liar, always scheming some deal and outlandish plan, a dreamer, an exaggerator, a perceived Soldier-of-Fortune, but not a doer, more of a punk.

"We've had Bob under surveillance for a long time because of his boasting of being a Freedom Fighter, planning on invading Nicaragua and displaying of guns." I thought it was uncharacteristic for him, but he told me Bob had rented a red Lincoln Continental automobile and with the FBI's informant, (I learned later the informant's name was Tom Bleming) went to Canada. Bob was sporting diamond rings, a fancy watch and had $6,000 on him. They met with a banker to enlist getting money to invade Nicaragua. Apparently they were unsuccessful. On the return, the FBI lost them near the U.S.-Canadian border.

Hard to believe losing a red Lincoln Continental, isn't it?

Tom concluded by saying, "Like you, we thought he wasn't anything but a dreamer and not a threat to the U.S. so we discontinued our surveillance.

Several days later, Tom Webber called me. He said a Sinikka Lawless from Norristown called him and said she had information concerning Bob Freels. He recommended that I call her. I did.

When I first spoke with Sinikka, she didn't divulge much. She said, she was friendly with Bob and Maureen and spent time talking with them in their apartment. Sinikka had gone through a kidnap-divorce episode which "nearly killed her." She now heads an organization for divorced women. She said Bob scared her; Maureen even expressed concern over Bob's "secret activities."

I had several phone calls with Sinikka, mostly chit-chat. However, she did put me in touch with Phyllis Watts and her son Tom Watts, who operate the CHILDREN RIGHTS OF PA, INC., an Allentown agency that helps find missing children. More about them later.

At 1:56pm, on August 7th, my wife's birthday, Maureen's mother, "Peg," called from Wellsboro, Pa. She said MAUREEN CALLED from Central America. Her sister, June, took the call. The word was that Wilkin, Freels and the boy were safe and doing well. The call had been placed by an operator with a Spanish accent. June said to Maureen, "Good to hear you're alive. Everyone is being hurt and everyone is looking for you." Maureen said she knew that and she would write and hung up.

In the forty five days Jimmy had been missing, it was the first indication Debbie, Mary Ann or I had that he was alive and apparently doing well. Also, this was the first clue they were out of the country. This changed my thinking somewhat because I and the people I was working with were still putting a lot of effort on what and how to deal with Bob in case he was apprehended in the states.

Two weeks after my first phone call to Sinikka Lawless, I received a call from FBI agent, Tom Webber. He told me to call Sinikka and ask about her boyfriend.

I did.

Sinikka had a meeting with Tom Webber and was undecided as to whether she should divulge to me everything she knew including her boyfriend's input. Webber's advice was to tell me the details and let me decide what to do with them. First, she apologized for not telling me everything she knew earlier, but would do it now

Sinikka and her boyfriend, Tom Bleming, knew about the abduction in advance! So the story goes——. "I feel so guilty for not stopping the abduction," she said. "I wanted to blow the whistle, but Tom told me not to get involved." Since the abduction, Tom and Sinikka had several arguments over the issue. Tom Bleming is a mercenary friend of Bob's and a Soldier of Fortune. Tom knew of Bob's plan and was part of it. He is the one that left the note on the bulletin board in the apartment saying he had a buyer for Bob's furniture The difference between them is that Tom was the FBI informant.

Sinikka was aware of Jimmy getting his vaccination in preparation of them leaving. "The day before they were to leave I got cold feet. I tried to call your daughter to warn her, but I didn't know her address or phone number. I knew the town where Debbie lived started with a 'W'. I looked in the phone book for Woodbury, Woodhaven, but couldn't think of Woodstown."

Sinikka told me Tom was a Vietnam veteran. He fought for the CIA in the Panama invasion several years ago. He was captured with 300 others and put in jail for two years. He was physically abused. Now he is bitter.

She said Tom was now living in Alabama. She gave me his phone number and I was not to call him until after 11:00 pm.

I did that the same night.

Tom Bleming verified what Sinikka had told me. In addition, he said Freels had conned him.

Freels told him that he had been a captain in the marines, had lots of money, had U.S. approval for his plan to invade Nicaragua, and had been a policeman in Nashville, Tennessee and his brother had been a police officer there also. All of which was a lie. Tom thought Freels was brilliant and convincing and his plan for invading Nicaragua came out of a "James Bond book."

A couple other things he said were, "I told the FBI in Philadelphia Jimmy was to be kidnapped." Maureen didn't know details of the "plan" he and Freels worked out.

This "plan" was for Freels to go to Costa Rica. "I suggested to Bob that they drive to Costa Rica on the Pan-American Highway. I gave them names of some contacts in the mountains near the Nicaraguan border. Once they got to Costa Rica, they were to proceed to the Thompson Ranch, where they would help them get established. My bet is they are in Costa Rica. If you need help, my buddy, Bill Carpenter, who fought with me in Panama, can get Jimmy back." This was the first news they may be in Costa Rica. There was a long pause, and Tom said, "Mr. Kuty, I'm afraid your grandson is in a lot of danger."

I got about two hours sleep that night.

CHAPTER 6

Introduced to Leo
Crampsey—A Godsend

My friend, Bill Cregar, invited me to his office on August 19, 1985 and introduced me to Leo Crampsey. Leo was retired from the State department after twenty five years of service and was now working for Bill and Du Pont. Leo and I worked in the same downtown office building. We became good friends and started going to lunch together each working day to discuss strategy.

Leo was a big man, over 6 feet tall, weighing 230 pounds. He was in his sixties with thick gray hair. His outstanding feature was his hardy laugh. He just stood out in a crowd.

I had been spending weeks trying to find out if Jimmy had a passport. I had talked with, and written to, the passport office in the state department office about this matter. They replied none was issued. Within two days, Leo found out a passport was issued and the number. After the passport office was contacted with this information, they confirmed it.

Among many of Leo's assignments with the State Department was being a Regional Security Officer (RSO) at the American Embassy in Guatemala, (1970-1973). He had intelligence contacts throughout Central America. This was amazing. Once he got involved, the doors started opening.

Leo wrote to all the RSOs in the Central American U.S. Embassies. He requested they check their country's immigration records to see if Bob and Jimmy Freels and Maureen Wilkin entered their country. It didn't take long, within two weeks, on September 25, 1985, one of Leo's connections in the U.S. Embassy in Guatemala called him with the first solid information that they entered Guatemala. HOORAY !

Surprisingly, the embassy contacted our prosecutor, Frank Hoerst. He and the Chief of Police, Walt Simpkins, were at my house when I returned home from work the day of the call to inform me of the events. I told them I already knew that Freels had been to Guatemala.

The question remained are they still there?

Jorge (pronounced Whore-hey) Luis Lemus, who worked in the Embassy's security office made the call. Jorge and Leo knew each other well. Leo was responsible for getting Jorge promoted through the ranks to his present position. Jorge was Guatemalan but could speak English fairly well.

Jorge had picked up a paper trail that showed the trio had driven through Mexico and into Belize in their 1985 Volvo. From there they took a ferry from Punta Gorda across the Gulf of Honduras, arriving the second week of July in Puerto Barrios on the east side of Guatemala. On their Visas they registered to stay until October 8, 1985.

He also learned they had spent a week or two at a grimy hotel in Puerto Barrios run by Gladys Smith. The hotel reportedly doubled as a whorehouse and whose clientele included mercenaries and local Police. Jorge presented pictures from posters to a maid who remembered seeing them.

Jorge immediately went to work and wrote to the Guatemalan National Police to put out an alert to stop them if they try to leave the country.

I hired an investigator, Eleazar Gomez Reyes, from the Cecil Nelson Detective agency, to work with Jorge Lemus, to try and track the Freels down.

On November 5th Jorge reported the investigator learned Bob had sold the Volvo on October 9, 1985 to a Lieutenant Colonel Mario Vinceo Gonzales. He is a member of the Guatemala army, therefore, does not pay taxes. The investigator learned this information through customs.

When Bob entered Guatemala he had to register his Volvo with Customs. The primary reason for this is, there is a large sales tax on sales of cars and Guatemala wanted this sales tax in case the vehicle is sold in the country. The only way to avoid this tax was that the military was exempt from this tax law.

When the investigator went to interview the Lieutenant, he would not divulge anything. No names or the fact he even bought the Volvo.

Another thing the Customs told the investigator, the Lieutenant only paid 50%, or about $6,000, of the agreement because Freels did not furnish the title.

Customs called Jorge and said; Bob, Maureen and Jimmy were to Immigration on November 8, 1985 to get their Visas extended. They needed more documentation and were to return on the 12th or 13th. This put everyone on "HIGH ALERT." Jorge had the Police, Customs and the Embassy poised to make an arrest. They said Maureen was on crutches with what appeared to be a broken foot or leg. They never showed.

Their trail went cold again.

CHAPTER 7

And then there was Michelle

There were two letters in the stack of mail left at Bob and Maureen's apartment in Norristown, Pa. that intrigued me. They were addressed to Jim Freels and were from Michelle Yomtov at 2363 Edgewater Terrace, Los Angeles, California. The letters were dated July 3 (hand written) and July 22 (typed), on their envelopes.

The first read:

> *Dear Jim,*
> *Please send me the photos you said you'd return as well as all other material pertaining to the fiasco.*
>
> > *Thank you,*
> > *Michelle*

The second letter was one full page typed and was impossible to make sense of. It started:

> *Dear Jim,*
> *Please help me:*

Then it read in part;

> *"I want my pictures back. I want all the material back I sent you. The beatings I had to take and my constant bleeding now surely merit that at least you keep that much of your word, don't they? I'm begging you not to use that stuff against me. I know that a person like you loves to be begged because that heightens your pleasure in betraying me."*

In conclusion it read:

> *"Please! God! Jim! Help me!*
>
> Michelle

A third letter came in the mail dated August 5, 1985 It was two typed pages with much of the same garbage talk.

I saved these letters not knowing what to do with them. My curiosity finally got the best of me.

On September 16, 1985, I wrote to Michelle. *"Michelle, I know Jim Freels very well. Like yourself, with your problems with the photos, he has caused me problems. Maybe we can help each other. If interested, call me. Jim Cootie, 609-769—."*

Well this opened a can of worms that I had a hard time closing.

Michelle called two days later. She was hysterical. After she got herself back together she repeated much of what she said in the letters. She stated Jim's mercenary friend, Don Maldonato, Bob was going to Costa Rica. Some other tidbits: She talked with Maureen in June, Bob was not in, and Maureen told her they were going out of the country and were taking Jimmy with them. Once she tried to get Jim (Bob) at Associated Securities, (where Bob worked prior to the abduction), but they told her he was fired. Note: Tom Bleming said to me, Bob told him they threw a big party for him. She rambled on about her life, her affairs with Mick McGrady, Martha Raye's, ex husband, and association with R. K. Brown the president of the SOLDIER of

FORTUNE magazine. I agreed to meet with Michelle in Denver, Colorado on October 2nd.

The episode went on with Michelle for several months. I finally decided she was crazy and a con artist and dropped her. I mention her mostly because she had input that Bob was going to Costa Rica.

CHAPTER 8

Christmas

The weeks leading up to Christmas were discouraging and depressing, but very active. There were no more sightings or positive results since November 8, 1985. A great deal of time was spent on communicating with key people like: Bill Cregar, Du Pont Legal Department; Leo Crampsey, my advisor at Du Pont; Jorge Lemus, Guatemalan Embassy; Tom Webber, Philadelphia FBI; Wayne Price, NJ Missing Person Unit; Frank Hoerst, Salem County Prosecutor; Walt Simpkins, Woodstown Chief of Police; George Mitchell, Costa Rica Embassy; even Michelle, the nut from California.

Debbie called Bob's parents on December 23, 1985. Bob's father said he talked with Bob about six weeks ago, which would of been mid November. He had no idea where they were, but did talk to Jimmy and everybody was ok. I passed this information onto "Peg", Maureen's mother. She cried. "Peg" had been having health problems and had been in and out of the hospital since this episode started.

Jennifer, my older daughter, called me and said, "Debbie and I had an argument at her house about Jimmy and she threw me out." Debbie said, "Nobody was doing anything, including Pop." This was very depressing. Debbie was feeling the strain like all of us, even more so. I could understand her feeling that way, but I was doing the best I could.

To add insult to injury—Two Secret Service agents stopped at Debbie's house, claiming she was responsible for Olympic metals costing $418 that she supposedly signed for, and were not paid for.

What happened was, on December 20, 1983, six months before they separated, Bob ordered on a Visa card, Olympic coins costing $418, from the U.S. mint in San Francisco, California. The coins did not come. On February 4, 1984 Debbie wrote to "Visa" asking the charges be dropped. Several days latter Debbie signed for a package at the post office for Bob. It apparently was the coins and Debbie didn't know it. I called the Secret Service, Mitch Price. Never heard another thing, except a letter stating the charges were dropped.

I wrote in my Journal, "Lousy Xmas!" "Miss you Jimmy."

The one bright spot during this period was working with an organization called "Children's Rights Of Pa. Inc." of Allentown, Pennsylvania. It was run by Phyllis and Tom Watts along with Tony Padrone.

Jane Leathersick, Maureen's friend introduced Debbie and me to them. They were great advisors. Tom and I went to Washington D.C. and met with many of the senators and congressmen from New Jersey and Pennsylvania to ask for their support. More importantly, Phyllis and Tom Watts arranged to have Jimmy's picture as a missing person put on over 100 TV stations in the South and Midwest. One of my colleagues from Du Pont, Lew Patrick, stopped in my office at work after Christmas and said he saw Jimmy's picture on TV in Atlanta, Georgia, during the holidays.

CHAPTER 9

John Cattle—Costa Rica

Phyllis Watts called Debbie at work on December 31, 1985 and said a John Cattle, the head of the American Freedom Fighters, called her indicating he could help Debbie find Jimmy. She gave him Debbie's phone number at work.

Debbie immediately called me at work to let me know of this new development. I, in turn, relayed the message to Leo Crampsey and Tom Webber.

One hour latter, John Cattle called Debbie.

Cattle, who supposedly had just come home from Costa Rica for the holidays, said he had seen Jimmy's picture on television in Camden, Tennessee and had located Debbie through Children's Rights. "I saw Freeley, (John Cattle always referred to Freels as Freeley), Maureen and Jimmy in June when they stopped in at the camp," Cattle said. "I'm shocked to learn Jimmy was abducted. Freeley led me to believe he had legal custody of the boy." He said "Freeley had a suitcase full of money and the people who gave it to him were also after him." He said several times, "He thought it was the Canadians who were after him." After talking to his wife, Cattle decided it was not in the interest of the child to be in Central America and would like to help. Cattle said he had more to tell us and hinted at a plan for getting Jimmy back. "Can you fly down to Nashville on Friday?" This was Tuesday. I said, "I'll be in touch with you."

This was the New Year Holiday and it was difficult getting in touch with anyone. I did speak with Leo Crampsey and Bill Creagar. Both were interested and both suggested I be cautious.

Debbie and I took off from Newark, New Jersey, airport at 10:45 Friday morning, January 3, 1986. A man with a bushy beard and red suspenders met us at baggage in Nashville airport and identified himself as Lee Wolfe. He took us to see Cattle who was sitting at one end of a lounge in the farthest corner on the second floor of the airport. Cattle was about my height, 5' 7". He was tanned and looked like most recruit's memory of their drill sergeant.

"Your son-in-law and daughter's husband is a dangerous man, you know," Cattle said. "He once had a girl in Los Angeles beat up. He's bright, but he'll do anything to get rich. From what I know, he's on his way to Costa Rica. And all three of them are in danger because they're unwelcome gringos."

He proceeded to tell us things, some of which, we already knew.

He said, "When Freeley stopped in June he told him to see Gladys Smith in Puerto Barrios." He added, "Gladys Smith was a 'hooker' and a 'lady' with women. She was married to a Canadian, was closed mouth and close friends with the police.

Bob told Cattle that he bought the Volvo and paid cash for it. Also, Bob took helicopter lessons. Cattle's comment was he didn't have enough lessons to fly a helicopter.

I asked him whether he thought Bob was involved in the drug trade, he said, "No". He also said he wasn't wise enough to the ways of the "traffic" to be involved.

Cattle said, "He didn't have any use for Bob in his organization. He was out of shape for field work and just didn't fit in."

Cattle said he was pretty sure where Bob was going in Costa Rica. "I can find him and rescue Jimmy for you. It'll cost you ten grand plus $5,000 for expenses. I need a notarized contract and the $5,000 up front, and I need an answer by tonight." He was supposedly leaving that night for Michigan and then to Washington D.C. for a couple days before returning to Central America. (I wrote in my journal notes, "He now sounds like a mercenary, not a humanitarian.")

After warning us not to inform American embassy officials in Guatemala and Costa Rica of the plan ("they'll leak it"), Cattle and Wolfe left.

When we got back home, Mary Ann said it was a chance we should take. It made Bill Cregar and Leo Crampsey nervous and neither liked the ransom, but they said it's up to me.

After the meeting with John Cattle, I was convinced he knew a lot about Bob and was his principal advisor on where to go and who to contact. His detailed knowledge of contacting Gladys Smith in Puerto Barrios and other things clinched it. Most of what he said we already knew through Jorge Lemus's investigation. We also knew Bob, Maureen and Jimmy were in Guatemala, but the question was, "Were they still there?" Several sources said they were told to go to Costa Rica.

Based on what I knew, I decided to take a $5,000 chance. I called John Cattle and said it was a go.

CHAPTER 10

The Trip to Costa Rica

On January 5, 1985, two days after meeting with John Cattle in Nashville he called. He requested that Debbie and I meet him at the Amstel Hotel in San Jose, Costa Rica, on January 12, 1986. "I'll contact you there. Plan to return on the evening of the 13th or 14th." He paused, "With Jimmy."

While waiting and trying to decide whether to go or not, I called all my advisors. None were encouraging, they all warned me of the pitfalls of the arrangement, but all said they would help if we decided to go.

Tom Watts, of the Children's Rights said, "Don't go! It could be a trap. Your son-in-law and Cattle could be in cahoots. They grab you and—poof!—they blow you away."

Leo Crampsey and I called the Costa Rica Embassy a couple of times. I spoke with George Mitchell, Jim Nagel and Kirk Katula. Their message was always the same. John Cattle is a "Drugs and weapons runner, a real dirt bag." They even expressed concern whether Immigration would let him in. (WOW). They urged me not to have anything to do with Cattle or his plan. I talked with Sinikka Lawless, her input was not to deal with John Cattle. Tom Bleming called me, he didn't like me dealing with Cattle and offered to go to Guatemala should I decide to go there.

I was now undecided, as what I should do, until I got a call from Bill Cregar on my 53rd birthday, January 8, 1986. He called both Leo

Crampsey and me into his office. He turned to Leo and asked him, "Leo, if I gave you a week off work, with pay, would you go with Mr. Kuty and his daughter to Costa Rica?" Leo never hesitated, "Sure would." I could hardly believe it! I immediately volunteered to pay Leo's expenses. This gracious act enabled me to make my final decision to go to Costa Rica. Having Leo as my interpreter, bodyguard and assist with the embassy was a **godsend.**

I hurriedly made flight arrangements for the three of us and vacation plans for Debbie and me. Also, had the contract with Cattle drawn by my attorney, Tom Van Wart.

I was then blessed with another stroke of luck.

Back in the fall, a friend of mine, Gary Calkins, at the Du Pont Savannah River Plant in Aiken, South Carolina put me in touch with Al Smith. Al, handled the security for United Fruit Company and oversaw all the refrigerated fruit boat shipments between South and North America. I spoke with him about going to Costa Rica. He was hesitant but asked when I was going. I told him and gave Al Smith our flight information. He said he would be in touch.

Two days before we left, Al called and said that he made plans to go to Costa Rica with us, as part of a business trip. He would fly to Philadelphia and meet us on the plane. He had a plan to get Jimmy out of Costa Rica legally.

John Cattle informed me, before we left, he had a contact in Costa Rica by the name of John Teaford. I was to call him if I needed to know of Cattle's whereabouts.

The plan was for Leo Crampsey to fly to Costa Rica one day ahead of Debbie and me to make sure the embassy was up-to-date and the arrangements were in order.

One day before Debbie and I were to leave, I called John Teaford to find out whether Cattle was still on schedule. I learned Leo and Cattle were scheduled on the same flight from Miami, Florida to Costa Rica, which was that day. This threw me into a panic. I visualized Leo and Cattle sitting together, and knowing Leo, who loved to talk, alerting Cattle that the embassy and a former government official were involved. I tried to contact Leo but could not.

Thank goodness that didn't happen.

On Saturday, January 11, 1986, Debbie and I boarded the plane in Philadelphia for our flight to Miami then to Costa Rica.

Al Smith met us on the airplane in Philadelphia. He proposed a scheme to get Jimmy out of Costa Rica "legally" once we got him. Al took us to the Ionosphere Club in the airport where we got our tourist cards. Al filled his card out using erasable ink. Once we got through customs with the stamped tourist card, he would erase his information and fill it in with Jimmy's. The scheme worked.

The passport plan was, once in Costa Rica, Debbie was to go to the embassy and claim she lost Jimmy's passport and wanted to apply for a temporary one. With a little help from Leo Crampsey and the embassy this plan also worked.

We were all set with the paperwork.

When we got off the plane in Costa Rica, Leo was waiting with three embassy armed security guards. One took all our papers. We, Debbie, Al and I, followed Leo and the other two security guards passed by everyone to the baggage claim. When we got to baggage, all the papers had already been stamped. Once Al got his luggage, the security guards picked up our luggage, surrounded us and walked us through some private doors. Debbie, Al and I were loaded into a taxi with the guards and Leo in another vehicle, leading the way to the Boganville Hotel, where Al was staying, then to the Amstel Hotel, where Debbie, Leo, I and maybe John Cattle were staying.

The street outside the hotel window at night was noisy. Cars with green and white (Areas) and red and blue (Calderon) flags were honking their horns and people were screaming and hollering for the upcoming presidential election on February 2nd. This was January 11th, I wondered what it would be like just before election?

The next day, Sunday, Leo invited Kirk Katula from the embassy to the hotel for lunch. Kirk, along with his wife, met with Leo, Al, Debbie and me to discuss the use of the tourist card that had Jimmy's information and having Debbie apply for a temporary passport for Jimmy, based on the fact she lost it. Kirk agreed this procedure was legitimate and the next day Debbie was to go to the embassy to fill out a sworn statement that the passport was lost.

At six o'clock that evening, Debbie and I met with Cattle in the Amstel lounge. The very first thing Cattle said, "You see that gray hair big gringo fellow sitting at the bar. Do you know him?" I said, "Yes." He said, "I met him at the bar last night and he told me he worked for Du Pont, I figured then he was with you. Once the cat was out of the bag, I had Leo join us in the lounge. Leo later told me last night while sitting at the bar, a man came in and sat beside him and introduced himself as "John Cattle". Leo said he nearly flipped.

Cattle said, Freeley was seen about 45 miles south of San Jose, but neither Maureen nor Jimmy was seen with him. Cattle was going into the countryside and would return in two days. If he didn't find Jimmy by then, he would go to Guatemala and check with Gladys Smith. We signed the $5,000 contract authorizing the payment and Cattle left.

We waited. And we waited some more.

When we next heard from Cattle he was in Guatemala. Well how about that!

The Guatemalan Embassy confirmed he was there. They reported that one evening he was drunk and boarded a plane to Honduras, Central America. When Debbie and I met with Cattle in Tennessee, he told us he didn't drink or smoke.

We never heard from him again.

Well, I blew that one, but the Costa Rica adventure was not quite over.

On one of the 'wait days', Debbie, Leo and I took a ride around Costa Rica in our rental auto. We visited many landmarks. We drove until we ran out of hard road and went some more. We were on dirt trails, fording streams and hoping by going forward we would come back to civilization. It was a good thing Leo could speak Spanish, because only the natives knew which way we could go. It took us six hours to go one hundred miles. It was a good thing we didn't break down. Debbie said that was the scariest ride she was ever on and that she never prayed so hard.

The next morning Leo Crampsey flew home, Debbie and I spent an extra day because we had airplane scheduling problems.

On our last day in Costa Rica, now knowing John Cattle had scammed us, I decided to find out how John Teaford was associated with John Cattle.

Debbie and I invited John to our hotel room. We found out he was a business man and was having a financial dealing with Cattle. I told him our story, including the Costa Rica Embassy's assessment of John Cattle and how he scammed us.

He nearly jumped out of his chair, and hollered, "That bastard, he was probably planning to scam me."

John Teaford was originally from Illinois but presently resides in Missouri.

At one time, John had a 50% interest in one of the largest frozen food factories in the world in Cuba. He helped design the factory which processed 100,000 pounds of frozen fish per day and 100,000 tons of ice per day. Then Castro took over and he lost everything. "Fortunately my wife was pregnant and was with her family in Missouri," he said. A good thing because he escaped Cuba under darkness with nothing.

He was appointed to President Roosevelt's advisory panel, was friendly with Truman and was on a board to access losses of American companies in Cuba.

He bought a fish freezing plant in Puerto Limon, Costa Rica in 1979. It employed eighty people and included five refrigerated boats to transport the frozen fish to the states.

A couple years ago, the Costa Rica government passed a law that the government was to take over 50% of all private businesses. He refused and shut down the plant. The government revoked his license. Now he was trying to sell.

This brings us to John Cattle. Teaford knew Cattle by the name of John Fairborne.

John Fairborne was the name Cattle used on his passport. Teaford thought Cattle was a CIA agent because he was so secretive. He also thought I was using the code word "KUTY" on my calls. It appeared Cattle wanted the boats to run drugs and guns.

John Cattle was negotiating with Teaford to buy his business. Their lawyers had papers drawn up and settlement was scheduled in a couple weeks.

After our session, Teaford realized this was a scam and said he was immediately canceling dealing with Cattle.

On Sunday, January 19th, after spending a week in San Jose, Debbie and I headed home, minus Jimmy.

Back to Square One!

CHAPTER 11

The Letters

The next four weeks dragged.

I went to Washington D.C. two times. Once with Tom Watts, of Childrens Rights, to meet with a representative of the Contras in the office of U.S. Representative, William J. Hughes of New Jersey. The same day I met with the Sandinista representatives of the Nicaraguan Embassy. Neither the Contras nor the Sandinistas ever came up with information on the elusive James Freels.

The second visit to Washington D.C. was with Valarie Sieford from a neighboring town of Woodbury, New Jersey, who had a missing child. We visited Senators Bradley, Lautenberg, Spector and Congressmen Florio and Kildee. We talked about things in general.

On February 17th, I called Maureen's mother, "Peg" Haner. She said, "I got a nice letter from Maureen last week. It was postmarked Orlando, Florida." She says, "Everyone is fine; it is very hot where they are; Jimmy has lots of friends; I think of Bevin often; and she's learning Spanish."

I asked her to send me a copy of the letter, and she said she would, but by the tone of her voice and replies to my questions, I didn't think she wanted to. She's holding something back, I thought.

While anxiously waiting to see Maureen's letter, I heard from Michelle from Los Angeles. It was a handwritten letter, which rambled aimlessly much like the letters she sent to me before. She was trying to sell me a letter purportedly from a mercenary, addressed to the forties actress, Martha Raye. The mercenary mentioned Bob meeting someone in Costa Rica in March. Michelle wanted $1,000 for the letter. I wrote her, I would send her $250, which I did, another $250 if the letter turned out to be genuine, and $500 more if it led to Jimmy's safe return.

I sent this letter, along with a handwritten letter she previously wrote me, to a handwriting expert. The handwriting expert concluded "both letters were written by the same person." I consoled myself with the thought that Michelle's con job had cost me a hell-of-a lot less than John Cattle's.

Although Michelle pestered me, I no longer dealt with her.

I called "Peg" Haner a couple times inquiring about Maureen's letter. She continued to give me excuses why she didn't send it.

On March 8, 1986, approximately 20 days after "Peg" said she would send me a copy of Maureen's letter, I called her again. I asked if I could come to her house in Wellsboro, Pennsylvania to pick up the letter with its envelope. Her reply astounded me. She said, "I don't want you to come to my house, I won't send you the letter or the envelope." She said, Maureen said in the letter, they did not kidnap Jimmy—Jimmy knew two months before they were going to take him.

She hung up on me.

MY HEART SANK!

I decided to visit "Peg" later.

March 14, 1986—HAPPY 9th BIRTHDAY, Jimmy, wherever you are.

On March 16, 2013, a Sunday, Mary Ann, Debbie, Dawn and I went to Wellsboro, Pa. When we got there at noon, "Peg" wasn't home, but was in church. We waited for over an hour, she didn't show so I left her a note and came home.

In the note I said, "we had been there." I also said, "If you don't want to help me, should I find Maureen, I would do nothing to help her or you."

This got a reaction. She called during the five and one half hour ride home. I returned her call. She was a lot more congenial but still reserved. We talked for about an hour. She informed me she had three letters, the first she got in November, another came about a month later and the last came in February. Maureen had sent two of the letters to a friend, who forwarded them to "Peg" without any address. After all this, "Peg" said she would send me copies of all the letters.

Thank God!

Had we received the previous two letters, a lot of time and money may have been saved.

"Peg" wrote me a letter along with Maureen's three letters. One could sense in her letter she was under stress and reprimanded me for threatening her. I certainly could understand her frustrations and reluctance to share the letters with me. She probably realized that I may be her only hope.

These letters were the breakthrough we needed.

LETTER #1—"PEG" TO ME

Tues March 18

Dear Jim and family

I hope these letters will help in some small way. This is all the information I have at this time and nothing to hide. You do not need to threaten me this way again. How do I know I can trust you? You are anxious to get your boy back. It's possible he does not want to come back, also Maureen. I would like to hear that from their lips first. May be this nightmare will come to an end. You know I wouldn't put it past Jim (Bob) to have gotten the money from you the $5,000 and maybe split it with some else.

I have a friend here in Wellsboro who has lived in Guatemala. He says their is so much wild country that no one would ever find them. People are very poor there. Also the fact they have electric and are working they are rich compared to the natives. I'm sure Maureen will take good care of little Jim. When I know anything I'll call you do like wise. Return my envelope.

LETTER #2—FRIEND TO "PEG"

Finally a chance to actually tell you what my life is like. It has been most difficult adjusting to the climate, so called friends being theives, the usual social & cultural problems—BUT FINALLY— We've come through with only a few minor scars. Our home is lovely-our friends are strong and we're finally being accepted.

I'll be teaching English & Music in a few weeks. (My new Casio electric piano is beautiful—a perfect birthday present from Jim (Bob).)

We have a Doberman, German Shepard and cat.

Doberman is pure, German is 1/2 pure and cat-Tang, is the best rat & mouse catcher ever.

I'm taking Spanish lessons-2-3 hours daily, writing music and pulling music off cassettes, writing my novel, reading, writing lesson plans for teaching and training dogs. The last one we trained took 1st place in his class & best male in the country.

You must do me a favor-

Please call my mother & tell her we are fine. Tell her I will write her when I can. 1-7?7-7?4-22??. Tell her I'm sorry. Better yet-Just send her a Xeroxed copy of this letter.

We are all healthy, and happy-

Little Jimmy seems to be a different person-very happy and content. Finally a normal little boy.

Later in November I'll be in contact with you again.

Until then-remember I love you all very much and I'm very homesick. I see the same sun and moon and that makes me feel closer.

Maureen Ann

LETTER #3—FRIEND TO "PEG"

It is Christmas and we're not together but there is a good reason now. Even though you are not here with us you are here! We are now part of this country and?? contents. Every day I think about you. I enjoy learning my Spanish and I enjoy my house much more this year. I made all my decorations for the tree! How pretty! I am teaching English and piano here at my house in the afternoon and the evening. In morning I teach at school. Jim (Bob) is working at our other school teaching security and self defense. No more mercenaries! Here the opportunity is great because no one has anything—If you have only a little you have a fortune.

Vinicio is now our president—nonmilitary. He is a good man an Abraham Lincoln type but there is so much undercurrent of Communism here with Nicaragua and EL Salvador so close that he probably will not be able to see his own accomplishments. He was a candidate from Democracia Christiana. This is a country of much violence, kidnapping, robberies, and murders—not for money for food! It is nothing to kidnap a child for $100 and killing him/her if the money is not delivered. We are so careful with Jimmy-although he looks like a native, and that helps.

Last week a little boy two houses away was playing with bombas (fire-crackers) and blew his fingers off. I wrapped his hand as tightly as possible and his mom took him to the hospital. It took 25 minutes to get there! His little brother had powder burns on his legs and his eye. I did fine and cleaned them all.

Last night was our Christmas party for our friends here. We have two other couples we are close with. We had food typica-tamales, tastados, jrjoles, plantanos con crenia. My two little girls that I give piano lessons to, played for their parents and did a perfect job. There are no pianos here only electric-which is fine. I sang our song-"Have Yourself—"&" cried.

We must be very careful not to disclose our address because Jimmy's grandfather has offered a big reward for his return. Jimmy will never go back—he is very happy and he has said he'll run away or kill himself if he has to go back. His Espanol is excellent and he smiles a lot. It make us happy to see him happy and contented with life.

My dogs grow daily. I have three and a cat, tang The dobermans are my pride and joy! My Maya hound is my cuddle bug. Tang is the nata/raton catcher. Sundance is now six months, Gizmo, four months and Cassidy is three and a half. They insist on eating the toilet paper and the Christmas tree. They don't want to be left home alone even for a minute-they get into mischief when I leave.

Jim and I are talking about adopting a little girl. We have more than many and the children are so destitute. We will soon be citizens here—then we can do as we wish. We have no car, no public transportation—you wouldn't believe it! But the main thing is that we are happy—a full family and what we have is ours-our friends are good and we have a new life-an honest, fullfilling life—together.

We wish you a happy new year and hope you and your families find joy and peace in all you do.

I love you both forever
TP3

P.S. We lived thru our first earthquake! A terrible feeling almost like you feel when you have had four or five hours at a bar and stand up for the first time. Everything moves but you don't move with it.

I'm sure they check the mail at my mothers house and check the telephone. More than anything—I'd like to speak to her and Bevin. In time—I must learn patience and hope they are alright. I love them both and think about them/worry about them and cry for them.

Please send a copy of this to my mom. I love her so much and I know she doesn't understand any of this. Somehow someday I'll tell her the entire story—for now—I love her and Bevin and always will. I miss them.

LETTER #4—MAUREEN TO "PEG

7 febrero 1986

Dear Mom,

We are alright! More than that, we are happy! I know I have caused you a lot of worry, pain and anger. I am indeed very sorry. We wanted a chance to start over again and we took the chance. Jimmy was not Kidnapped! He knew of our plans two months before we left and he told no one! He wanted to be with us and to be happy normal little boy. He deserved it.

Our home is lovely but at this point I can't disclose where it is because we are not yet citizens. Soon I will tell you. My Spanish improves every day and I find their language very beautiful. Jimmy has learned faster than either of us but children usually do! We are both working. I am teaching English and music and Jim teaches self defense.

This country is incredibly beautiful but incredibly poor. The Indians (natives) still make it a very backward country thru lack of education and superstitions. The natives are about 70% of the population. I mean grass shacks rice and beans, no electric, no running water and many children, too many children. There are very few public schools here maybe 150 in the entire country. The rest are private and here, no education is free. I teach English in my house for 30.00 a month per student to professionals who are interested. Now I have one doctor and one lawyer. My piano students are my pride and joy! I have adults and children. Music here is taught differently, it's very confusing. Our American method is much better.

Besides our other occupations we raise Dobermans. I've sent other letters to you with some of the same information. If it's boring I apologize. Here in this country almost the 30% of the population has maids. I have one too. All the houses are built with a separate bedroom and bathroom for the maid. She cleans the house, cooks, washes cloths (by hand) and helps us at the market so others don't take advantage of us because we are Gringos. Only the very rich have wash machines here—too expensive, no service repairs and no extra parts.

I find it very hard to believe that it is February and still about 75 degrees. The nights are very cold but the days are lovely only there is no rain. We expect rain to start in April. We've had one shower since November, only a short one. Everything looks brown and very dry. Now there are many brush fires here.

Also we have many small earthquakes (tremors) if you have never been in a earthquake you are lucky. Our volcanos are active and absolutely beautiful. When I walk my dogs in the mornings I can see them spit and sputter.

Our friends are very special. We are comfortable and Jimmy has many, many amigos.

Every day I think of Bevin. I know she's okay with Jim and Diane. They are good parents for her. I didn't do this to hurt Bevin. I loved her enough to give her a full family. I will always love her. She's better off with them. I have a full family and she does too. Time will heal her, you and me.

I now have a good marriage and a lasting relationship. We have been thru a lot together and worked hard together. We have a comfortable life.

Until I write again, I love you very much.

Maureen

When I shared these letters with Leo Crampsey and Bill Cregar, Leo blurted, "They are near Guatemala City." The only active volcano in Central America is on the outskirt of Guatemala City, they just elected a new democratic President and they recently had a earthquake.

We concluded they had been living in Guatemala—undetected—for almost seven months and had never left there to go to Costa Rica or anywhere else. It also sounded like Bob had given up on the half-baked scheme he had been cooking before he passed into Central America. At least, I hoped he had.

After Leo and Bill finished reading the letters, Leo looked me right in the eyes and said, "Jim your going to have to go to Guatemala yourself. You're the only one that has the motivation and drive to find them."

So the saga began!

Both Leo and Jorge suggested I go to Guatemala over Easter. During Easter, Guatemala shuts down and everyone celebrates by having parades.

CHAPTER 12

To Guatemala

I visited the Du Pont Savannah River Plant and met with the Wackenhut Security Leader, John Evans. He advised me not to go because it would be a dangerous mission, but did offer to provide help. He contacted the Wackenhut International Service, who had offices in Guatemala City. He arranged for me to have two Wackenhut employees (detectives) at my disposal. Their names' were "Manuel" Flores Sanchez and Jaime "Roldolfo" Maran Segura. This was another stroke of luck. Only Roldolfo could speak a little English.

Talked with Jorge Lemus, he made arrangements for me to stay at the Camino Real Hotel. The United States Embassy told him not to help me, he said things have changed here. Jorge offered to do undercover work for me at night. I was disheartened.

Two days before I was to leave for Guatemala on March 26, 1986, Jerry Wilson from the U.S. Embassy called me at work and said, "Don't come. We will not help you." This was not only disheartening, it was shocking. All this after months before, the embassy being so helpful, promising to have Bob arrested, and put away for a long time. I couldn't believe it. Who will help me if one's own government won't?

Leo and I decided I would go anyway.

Now I had a great deal to do in preparation for the mission.

I got the airline tickets, prepared many pamphlets, purchased Spanish language cassettes. I didn't want Bob or Maureen to detect me should I bump into them, so I bought a disguise kit. It consisted of a wig, beard, mustache and tan makeup. I dyed my nearly white hair black.

My Disguise

CHAPTER 13
PART I

Guatemala—30 Days of Hell

Days One through Five

DAY 1.

Wednesday, March 26, 1986, playing a long shot, I boarded an Eastern airline from Philadelphia, Pennsylvania to Miami, Florida, then another Eastern flight to Guatemala City. My mouth was dry, and I had an empty feeling in my stomach, I wasn't at all elated. I was wondering if I weren't on another wild goose chase. I felt very uncomfortable going into a strange land not being able to understand or speak the language. All I knew, I had to do something.

On the flight from Miami to Guatemala City the second most important event happened to help me to find Jimmy. A Guatemalan lady sat down beside me. We struck up a conversation. She spoke excellent English. Her name was Susan Rodgers and was a travel agent for Clark Tours. She asked, "Why are you going to Guatemala?" "I'm going to try and find my grandson," then I told her my story. I showed her Maureen's letters, and she said, "They are around Guatemala City. "This chance meeting was a huge stroke of luck, some called it <u>Divine Intervention.</u>

Her brother, Andy Rodgers, was very influential in Guatemala, she told me. He was the manager of the Camino Real Hotel, same hotel

Jorge booked for me. What a coincidence. "It is Easter, and for the next four days the country will be shut down. On Monday morning you go see my brother, he'll be in the Hotel," Susan said.

Susan told me her family was very well to do, her mother, Evelyn, owned a brewery among other things. She was one of eight children. Susan was full of ideas and suggestions. For example, she gave me names of places that raised Dobermans and the name of a veterinarian who specialized in treating Dobermans.

Jorge met me at the airport that night. Jorge drove the rental car, that was in my name, to the Camino Real Hotel where the two Wackenhut detectives, Manuel Flores Sanchez and Jaime Roldolfo Maran Segura were waiting. Jorge read Maureen's letters to the detectives, We worked out a plan, Jorge did most of the interpreting. For the next four days the detectives and I would attend the parades and visit Indian villages, then after Easter investigate piano stores and veterinarians.

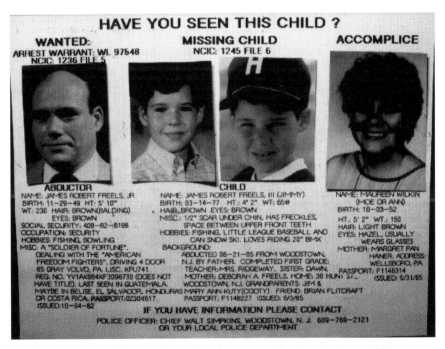

Poster given to the sheriffs in the Indian villages

DAY 2.

I awoke at 5:00am the next morning, kind of excited, but apprehensive. I spent considerable time putting my disguise on. I only wore the disguise when I went out into the public. Rodolfo, the detective that could only speak a little English, what a pair we were, met me at the hotel where we had breakfast. We were to meet Manuel in Antigua.

On the way westward around Antigua, we passed through several Indian towns like San Antonio, San Pedro and they were horrible—dusty roads and shacks. I didn't see any gringos, and I said a silent prayer, "God, please don't let me find Jimmy living amidst this squalor."

At noon, we met with Manuel and attended the start of the Easter festivities in Antigua. For hours I looked into thousands of faces, a few of them were white. None of them were Jimmy's!

That evening, I took Roldolfo home. Roldolfo had no phone, no TV, no vacation and worked seven days a week.

Later that evening, I phoned Jorge, Mary Ann and Susan Rodgers. Susan asked me to call her every day to keep her informed. Susan said she would get Jimmy and me on a plane and out of the country on a moments notice.

DAY 3.

Things started to go downhill.

The detectives and I returned to the same general area. As usual it was hot. Instead of my disguise allowing me to blend into the crowd, it was causing people to stare at me. My makeup started to streak from perspiration. I guess I looked neither Indian nor gringo. It also aroused the suspicion of at least one Guatemalan policeman who stopped the trio of us and wanted to know what we were doing. He checked our credentials. When he compared my passport of a slightly balding, gray haired gringo to my apparently, black haired, bearded, poor disguise, I knew I was in trouble. During the interrogation, the crowds started to circle us to see what was happening. I was scared. Thank heaven, Manuel Sanchez and Rodolfo Segura were able to convince the policeman that I was on the up-and-up, only after they had me take my wig and beard off, making me look more like the picture on the passport. The policeman released me and the crowd dispersed.

I honestly thought I was going to jail. If you go to jail in Guatemala, you're done. First, the conditions of the jails are so deplorable, one might not survive and second, once in jail they may keep you a very long time for no good reason.

Day 4.

Saturday, was just more of the same. A lot of walking. We visited Lake Amatitlan, stopped to see the Chief of Police—no gringos. Went to San Antonio, they were having "Hood Days". Ended up in Antigua again.

That night I went to bed beat and terribly discouraged. I also started to feel bad.

I think the next day was one of the worst days of my life.

Day 5.

The next morning, Easter Sunday of the adventure, I awoke with the curse of "Montezuma's Revenge." A bad case. If one doesn't know what Montezuma's Revenge is, it's diarrhea. If that wasn't bad enough, I was developing blisters on both feet.

I should not have gone with Roldolfo that day, but I did. We went into those God-awful towns where the filth and stench were compounded by drunks sleeping off their celebration of the Resurrection along the side of the road. We continued to observe the parades, but found nothing. Between potty breaks, I walked through the crowds staring so hard my eyes ached. No Jimmy.

The search expanded into the Indian villages around Guatemala City. We went to several jails in that surrounding area, passed out leaflets, and talked to the sheriffs. Half of them were drunk, and the jails were atrocious, but we did it. I was constantly running to their outside toilets, which were often just large buckets half full with water, and were God-forsaken places.

In all these places, like Antigua, where we talked to the police chief who told us that the San Felipe police reported us, and at the markets in San Lucas, San Miguel, San Felipe, or at Ciudad Viejo in the shadow of volcano Fuego, the response was always the same, "No gringos."

I wasn't sure which malady would kill me first, the runs or the giant blisters on my feet. After opening the blisters and taking Pepto Bismo for the diarrhea, I went to bed at eight o'clock.

A Bad Easter.

CHAPTER 13
PART II

Days Six through Twelve

"We found Jimmy"!

DAY 6.

Monday morning, a day after Easter, with my bowels still doing flip-flops, and Guatemala getting back to normal, I met with Andy Rodgers in his office. Andy was in his early thirties, about 5 foot 7 inches, a little stocky, but was a little lighter skinned than most Guatemalan's.

I didn't even have to introduce myself, Susan, his sister, who I met on the airplane, had told him everything.

Andy Rodgers took over and was another **godsend**.

That morning while Andy and I were talking, one of the detectives, Rodolfo Segura, went to check the music stores to see if a piano was purchased by the Freels.

The first thing Andy did was change my name on their records, to Jim Oswald, my mother's maiden name. He took my money and put it in the hotel safe.

I told Andy that the Freels entered Guatemala through Puerto Barrios, and stayed in a hotel, managed by a lady named Gladys Smith. She was married to a Canadian and based on what Jorge Lemus of the U.S. Embassy knew, she was in Canada. Andy said, "Let's find out." He phoned the Canadian Embassy, he knew someone there. They confirmed this strange lady, Gladys Smith, was there and they had her under surveillance.

I told Andy, Bob had entered Guatemala with a new 1985, gray Volvo, and Pennsylvania license plate number KPU741. Andy said, "There is only one Volvo dealer in Guatemala City." He immediately called them. A mechanic remembered servicing a gray Volvo with a Pennsylvania license about five months ago, but they had no address of the owner. The mechanic recalled the owner, who fit Bob's description, insisted on keeping the service record.

As Andy and I were talking, the leader of an Israeli Swat team, URAY, who was staying at the hotel, visited us. The Swat team's mission was to protect the country's new President, Vinico. He surprised both Andy and me because he had a pamphlet on Freels and was semi up-to-date on the case. (Looks like Susan Rodgers was at work again). Once URAY was convinced I had legal rights to Jimmy, he came up with a plan to get Jimmy out of the country.

URAY told me, "Once Jimmy was located, the Swat team would pick him up, I was to go to Mexico City and they would deliver him there." I tentatively turned him down fearing legal complications. I told him, "I prefer to get him out legally, but should that fail I would be in touch with him." URAY kept in touch with me in the following weeks.

Later that morning, after talking with Andy Rodgers, I walked to the U.S. Embassy, which was only several blocks away, with an uneasy feeling. This was my first contact, since leaving home, with the directive from the Embassy not to come to Guatemala. I met with Jerry Wilson, Jorge's boss, who had been most cordial when I talked to him on the phone last fall and early spring. He didn't even invite me into his office. He kept glancing from side to side as though he was afraid to be seen talking to me. "I don't think we can do much for you, Jim," he said coolly.

I couldn't figure it out. What the hell had happened? I speculated that before the recent election, under the ousted dictator, the American Embassy had had a free hand to do almost anything, and now the new government had told our guys to keep their freakin' hands off internal affairs.

Late that morning, Rodolfo reported no one in the music stores had seen nor recalled selling the Freels a piano.

Manuel Sanchez then joined Rodolfo and me in the early afternoon to review veterinarians' addresses. One of whom may have treated Bob's dogs. I spent most of my time listening to the two detectives conversing in Spanish. It was a real strain.

I was feeling terribly alone. I was still fighting the dysentery.

Having come up with no good leads after five and half days of searching, I feared the detectives were losing enthusiasm for the case.

"Oh God, what am I going to do if they leave me?" I thought. "They are the only thing I got going for me down here."

The three of us then went to check the veterinarians. The second one we visited was a "BINGO." Rodolfo and I sat in the car while Manuel went in to talk with the veterinarian, his name was Dr. Juan Ricardo.

When Manuel came out, he asked through Rodolfo, whether I would be willing to pay 100 quetzals, about $38, for information. "Of course," I told them, I gave Manuel the money. He went around to the back of the office. He returned to the car in about fifteen minutes, talked excitedly to Rodolfo in Spanish. I didn't know what they were saying. This communication gap was driving me crazy.

As we drove back to the hotel to find someone to interpret for me, Roldolfo kept saying to me, "Everything OK, everything OK." Andy Rodgers was to be my interpreter.

This was Manuel's report: The veterinarian recognized Bob from the poster and said he treated his dog, Sundance. He WOULD NOT disclose Bob's address because Bob had threatened him physical harm if he did. However, Manuel used the 100 quetzals to bribe one of the vet's workers to look into files and get Bob's address, which he did. HOORAY!!

Another twist.

Manuel was Rodolfo's supervisor and headed the Wackenhut Office in Guatemala City. After we got to the hotel, Manuel balked in talking with Andy Rodgers or giving the address of Bob's residence to either Andy Rodgers or me. Only after persuading Manuel to talk to the U.S. Embassy's Jorge Lemus, would he talk with Andy.

Manuel would not, however, give the address to Andy or me. He said, "Tomorrow Rodolfo and I will go to the residence and verify and make sure they are living there. If they are, I will give you the address tomorrow."

I talked with Mary Ann sharing the good news. She told me Debbie, Jimmy's mother, started a new job with Mannington Mills, a local floor covering manufacturer. This was good news because it paid more than the bank job and had excellent benefits. I also shared Jimmy's good news with Susan Rodgers, Jorge Lemus, and the next morning with Leo Crampsey. Jorge suggested I talk with Larry Kerr at the U.S. Embassy. I did. Larry suggested that I come see him the next morning.

Had to take Sominex to get to sleep that night. Went to the bathroom all night. I was still a sick puppy.

DAY 7.

Tuesday, Andy Rodgers and I met, and he started to make arrangements to find me a lawyer. I told Andy I had talked to Leo Crampsey the night before. Andy said, "Well how about that, I dated Leo's daughter when they were living here." Leo later told me to tell Andy, "Cathleen was married and living in Brunswick, Maine." Leo also said, "Andy's mother Evelyn ran a school and his children went there. She was formally a wealthy Castille."

That morning, I went to see Larry Kerr at the Embassy. I had spoken to Larry several times before I came to Guatemala. Fortunately, Larry was softening his recent rigid stance towards me. Jerry Wilson, Jorge's boss, was not softening his stance and continued to be obstinate. Larry heard about our good news and thought getting a lawyer was a good idea. He thought working through the family court was good too. He did offer to talk to whatever judge was assigned since he knew most of them. I was pleased with his attitude.

At 10:45 that morning Manuel and Rodolfo picked up my car keys and left looking for the Freels using the address they got from the vet's office. I stayed behind at the Camino Real Hotel, nursing blisters on my feet from Indian village searches, and the remaining dysentery, until they returned. I was having anxiety attacks, imagining everything that could go wrong. But I was wrong, I had to conclude these detectives were professionals, because at four o'clock they returned and said they found the house and they were living there. Hallelujah!!

Their story was: They had a hard time finding the area. It was in a fairly decent suburb, west of Guatemala City, not too far from where Rodolfo lives. On the street where they lived was a small store, they talked with a young girl and impersonated themselves as looking for a piano teacher that they thought lived nearby. The girl pointed to the house. It was the address they had of the house. She casually mentioned they were gringos and had a young boy living there and with a little talk she indicated he often rides his bike up and down the street.

They then went to the house with the intention of signing one of their children for piano lessons. Neither Bob nor Maureen were there but an older Indian maid answered the door. She said, "The man and woman of the house were at a local Country Club playing tennis." Manuel and Rodolfo went to the Country Club and from the car saw two people who fit the description of Bob and Maureen playing tennis. The detective's work was now done. I offered to pay them, but they insisted I stop at their office to make the payment and they would furnish Bob's address.

THIS WAS THE MOMENT I WAITED SO LONG FOR. I COULDN'T BELIEVE IT! I CALLED HOME AND TOLD MARY ANN, DEBBIE AND LEO CRAMPSEY THAT **"WE FOUND JIMMY!"**

Being alone in my hotel room, still not feeling well, and 4,000 miles from home, that night **I broke down and cried.**

This would be a good place for this adventure to end, but it didn't. The next twenty three days, of the 30 days in hell, were just as hard, if not harder than the previous seven days.

Later that evening, Andy called me to his office and said, "I made arrangements for you to see a lawyer. You are to meet with her tomorrow morning at 8:30am in the Pan Am building in Guatemala City. Her name is Maria Louisa Beltranena, a former Justice of the Supreme Court, presently teaching at a Catholic University and she can speak fluent English."

See what I meant when I said, "Andy Rodgers took over."

Day 8.

Wednesday, April 2, 1986. I drove to the Pan Am Building on 6th Avenue in Guatemala City. Not knowing how to read street or parking signs, it wasn't easy. I pulled into what I thought was a parking lot and a youngster, maybe twelve years old, asked for my keys. I was reluctant and didn't know what to do. Just then a young man about twenty two years old passed by, he was carrying a backpack, looked like a student and could speak English. I asked him, "If it was okay for me to give the boy the keys?" he said, "Yes he was the attendant." I then asked him where the Pan Am Building was on 6th Avenue. He actually took me there. He wouldn't take anything for his efforts, except a "Thanks." The saga wasn't over.

When I got to the building I couldn't find the stairs, but there was a semi-open elevator. The lawyer's office was on the third floor. Shortly someone came by, opened the elevator door themselves, stepped in, closed the door, and went up. I did the same thing but went up and down twice before I figured how to stop and get off.

Maria was an elegant Guatemalan lady who spoke fluent English. I learned later she was educated at Princeton University. After hearing my story, she agreed to take my case, but warned that the Guatemalan government's legal system had changed and this would be her first experience. She would have to get the Family Court to issue a court order giving me custody of Jimmy. She told me to be prepared to have to get additional papers like "Power of Attorney" and have them certified by the Guatemalan Embassy in New York City. She would need documentation to insure the safety and welfare of Jimmy. She would call me when she found out what was needed by the judge.

On the way back to the hotel I stopped at the U.S. Embassy on 6th Avenue to talk to Larry Kerr. I brought him up to speed. Larry said that he would send an assistant when Jimmy was picked up to insure the welfare of Jimmy. He gave me the address of the Guatemalan Embassy at 57 Park Avenue, NY, 10016. The Consulate General there must approve the legal papers.

At the hotel, I met with Andy Rodgers. I told him what the lawyer, Maria, said. He said, "He knew the Consulate General."

While talking to Andy, Maria called. Andy took the call. She said, the judge of the Family Court wanted: 1) The papers that granted custody to Deborah Freels, my daughter, Jimmy's mother; 2) Documentation that I had been given Power of Attorney to act on my daughter's behalf and; 3) He wanted certification that the New Jersey lawyer who handled the custody proceedings was a practicing attorney in good standing. The custody papers must be certified and all papers registered with the Guatemalan Embassy in New York City by the Consulate General.

It was a tedious process that drove me to the limit.

I told Andy, to accomplish all this, my wife in New Jersey will have to get the custody papers from the Salem County Court House and have them certify them, the Power of Attorney, from our lawyer Tom Van Wart and certification that he was in good standing.

Andy turned to me and asked, "Where is your wife?" I said, "Working." He said, "He would call her and you tell her what she must do."

When I talked to Mary Ann her question was, "When can I do all this?" I said, "You are to leave your job NOW and get started." She did.

Andy, then called the Consulate General in New York City, Antonio Aris de Castille (Andy knew his brother), and arranged to have them expedite Mary Ann's papers. It didn't quite work that way.

Later that afternoon, I went to the Wackenhut office on 8th Avenue, not far from the hotel, to pay for Manuel Sanchez and Rodolfo Segura's services. Manuel was not available, so I paid a Fernando Hagel, the son the President of Wackenhut International. Fernando told me, John Evans, of the Savannah River Plant in South Carolina, was there in 1983 to help them find his brother who had been kidnapped. I wrote Wackenhut a check for 1,000 quetzals or about $380. That's all they wanted, and I was more than satisfied. Wackenhut then gave me the house location as: Locate 2 Calle Lote 4 Manzana G, Siccion 1 Pinares de San Cristobal. Wackenhut's work was now done. I then got together with Andy Rodgers and gave him the address of the Freels. Andy said, "I know exactly where they live. I was involved in the development of that area."

Andy immediately called the survey office for a detailed map of the development. They sent it to his office by messenger. He pointed to the house where they were living on the map. He made arrangements with, URAY, a Swat team member (Benny), me and himself to visit the area the next day.

DAY 9.

The next morning, Mary Ann, along with my sister, Irene, and her husband, Martin Mlinek, the three of them hustled to the Guatemalan Embassy in New York City, one hundred and ten miles from Woodstown, New Jersey. They parked the car on the outskirts of the city, and took a taxi, because they didn't know the exact location of the embassy and to beat the traffic. The embassy would not accept the custody papers because only the first page of the custody order was notarized and they wanted every page notarized.

Mary Ann called me and asked, "What should I do?" I said, "Hurry back to the Salem County Court House and get all the pages certified and notarized and get back to the Guatemala Embassy today." They did it, but I don't know how. They got back to New York City late. The Consulate stayed over to accept the papers. But the embassy still wouldn't accept the papers because the "Power of Attorney" was not notarized. One would think they would have been told this on the first visit. Everyone in the Salem County Courthouse thought the lawyer's signature on the Power of Attorney would be sufficient. When I talked to Mary Ann that evening, she said the papers would be at the embassy in the morning. Because of this charade, we lost two precious days plus the weekend.

Andy got in touch with me in the afternoon to go to San Cristobal, Freels' address. Even that wasn't easy.

I put on my disguise, went to the lobby and got picked up by the hotel security and they wouldn't release me (Andy had gone to get the car). They couldn't understand me. Finally, Benny, the Swat team member, came along and bailed me out.

I then joined URAY, Benny and Andy for the drive in Andy's bulletproof car out to where Jimmy was living. My heart was in my mouth. We drove past the house a couple of times and also a nearby school, where I pictured my grandson, the little gringo, sitting among Indians all speaking Spanish. The development was nice, at least Jimmy wasn't living in squalor like I saw in the Indian villages. Thank God they were living well.

Then we went to the tennis court. Sweet Jesus, there was Bob sitting with his back to the road watching a woman, believed to be Maureen, playing. I had never seen Maureen before but she looked like the pictures I had of her. The bald headed—SOB—was tanned and fit while here I was losing pounds by the day from dysentery and looking like Marley's ghost under this beard and mustache.

I was feeling elated having seen Bob and Maureen, but what goes up must come down. And it did as one will see later.

Wachenhut called and said I owed them a couple more dollars because the exchange rate changed. No problem, I took care of that.

Day 10.

Friday. **The diarrhea stopped!** What a relief!

Mary Ann delivered the papers to the Guatemala Embassy in New York and they were approved. She air mailed them and I should receive them this weekend.

I talked with Jerry Wilson at the U.S. Embassy. I requested Jorge Lemus be permitted to talk with the Mixco Chief of Police to explain the sensitivity and possible danger of picking up Jimmy and Bob. Jerry said he didn't want to get Jorge involved because the embassy may do something that may lead to a lawsuit which would embarrass the embassy. He recommended Larry Kerr to be the contact person. Jerry said, "He is as responsible for Freels and me, being we both are U.S. citizens." What a contrast in philosophy from before I came to Guatemala. They said then Bob would be picked up, maybe by them, and jailed. Oh well!

Day 11 and 12.

Saturday and Sunday. Weekends are not very productive, but the legal papers did arrive from New York via Eastern Airlines Saturday evening. The Eastern Airline manager expedited me to obtaining the package quickly. I spent most of Sunday unwinding, but I did call Maria to inform her I received the legal papers. She requested that I have them to her office at 8:30am Monday morning.

Left a message with Rodolfo to call me. I wanted to give him the fifty dollar tip I offered him.

CHAPTER 13
PART III

Days 13 through 26

The Waiting Game

DAY 13.

The first thing Monday morning, April 7, 1986, I delivered the papers to Maria at her office. It was then she told me all the papers had to be translated into Spanish. WOW. She said she would get her students at the University to do the translation and typing. She asked for 100 quetzals or approximately $38.00. I paid her.

Now we have to wait! And wait! And wait!

Before I went to Guatemala, my closest friend and skiing buddy, J. Hamilton (Ham) Fowser, said he had a missionary friend, Roy Nelson and his wife Ethyl, who lived in Guatemala City. They were associated with the, "United World Mission", out of St. Petersburg, Florida. When I got there I called them and made arrangements to visit. We met often for lunch and on occasions for breakfast or dinner. I visited their home. They were the only American contact I had. They remained friendly during my entire stay in Guatemala. For their friendship I am grateful.

Needless to say, I maintained a dialogue with everyone almost daily while waiting for the legal papers to be translated into Spanish.

Developed another bout of dysentery. Not as bad this time and it was over in two days.

Rodolfo returned my previous day call. I invited Rodolfo to my hotel room to ask him if he would go with me to see if Jimmy was at the house and to give Rodolfo a tip of $50.00. No one yet had seen Jimmy. He came, but was very reluctant to take the tip. He finally took the tip, only after I told him that in America it's a custom to reward someone for doing a good job.

DAY 14.

April 10, 1986, I'm starting to climb the freakin' walls. Jimmy during this time still had not been seen and I was getting more and more nervous. I called Leo Crampsey in Delaware and expressed my feelings. He recommended I call a colleague of his, Cecil Nelson, who Leo helped set up a detective agency in Guatemala City when he was in the U.S. Embassy there in the 1970's.

I called Cecil and he came to my hotel room right away. I relayed my story and asked if he could put surveillance on Bob's house to see if Jimmy was there.

When I mentioned this to Andy he wasn't pleased. He was concerned too much activity might tip Bob off.

Rodolfo called and said he wouldn't be able to go with me to see if Jimmy was there. Again, I told him he was to keep the tip. I admired Rodolfo for backing out: I could sympathize with him to feel he may be putting his job in jeopardy.

DAY 15.

On Wednesday, Maria called me to her office. She wanted some background information on Bob to give to the judge. I delivered it promptly.

Cecil Nelson called and said, "He put two young employees in the area. They pretended to be 'lovers'." They parked their rear ends in the neighborhood. They reported, "The maid came out, but not Jimmy." They also reported a lot of police in the area, so they backed off.

Day 16.

The 'lovers' reported again. They saw Bob come out of the house and sit in a small Hyundai truck parked in front of the house. Several minutes later <u>Jimmy came out</u>. He rode his bike about a half hour. Bob got out of the truck and they both went into the house. For the first time we now know Jimmy is with them and doing fine, but the report infuriated me. It seemed like Jimmy was being held under lock and key like a prisoner. I thought, that's a terrible way the boy has to live. This resolved my determination to get him home to my daughter. It appeared like Jimmy was not going to school and they are very cautious with him.

The 'lovers' reported later that day Bob came out of the house and went to a house a block away known to be occupied by mercenaries.

After the fact, Cecil told me, the police activity in the area was a result of a recent kidnapping and murder. The police had found an unlicensed vehicle in that area which they believed to be associated with the kidnapping incident.

Day 17.

Woke up at 1:00am, couldn't sleep. Took Sominex at 2:30am. Woke up groggy.

After several calls to Maria regarding the legal paper translation to Spanish, I was getting anxious as to why it was taking so long. Finally, on the 17th day, Friday, Maria said the papers were ready. Monday, she would see the judge, except she was having a problem getting the Power of Attorney recorded in court. Lord what next, I thought.

Late Friday night, Cecil brought a written report to me at the hotel regarding the 'lovers' observations of the Freels' residence. I asked him how much I owed him, he said, "A handshake, any friend of Leo Crampsey was a friend of his." This touched me and I lost control of my emotions. I insisted I give him something, he reluctantly agreed to $38.00. He left.

In my lonely room I cried. There are a lot of special people out there, Cecil is one of them.

DAY 18 AND 19.

The weekend was uneventful. I did take a dip in the hotel pool. Ate at McDonalds for $1.00. The giggly waitresses made me point to what I wanted because for some reason they could not understand me.

Mary Ann said she filed for an Income Tax extension.

One luxury I had at the hotel was a TV. It had four English speaking channels. I was able, on occasions, to watch the Philadelphia Phillies and Flyers, and CNN.

DAY 20.

Monday. Here we go again. I finally contacted Maria in early afternoon: she hadn't filed the papers with the judge yet. The papers were ready but another hurdle occurred.

Who had jurisdiction, either Mixco, the district they lived in, or Guatemala City? She said, "If Mixco has jurisdiction, she may have to see another judge.

I started calling; Andy Rodgers, not in; Jorge Lemus, he thought Mixco; Larry Kerr, he wasn't sure but he did say, "I don't think Mixco has a Child Custody Court," I'll be damned, I don't either, I thought to myself. I felt whipped, mentally exhausted, frustrated, and wondering how long was this going to go on.

At 7:00pm, Maria called. I passed on Larry Kerr's comment. She said, "I'm going to the judge in Guatemala City tomorrow, I expect the judge to issue the court order and the Mixco Police to pick up Jimmy. Bob will be "extradited." Sounds good but we will see.

Note: The United States attacked LIBYA today.

DAY 21.

Tuesday, April 15, 1986. Income Tax Day.

The judge has the papers according to Maria. He will review them and <u>hopefully tomorrow</u> he will issue a Court Order.

I alerted everyone. Susan for airline tickets, Andy for assistance to the airport, and Jorge maybe to help when picking up Jimmy. Jorge said, "Jerry Wilson was in Panama and for me to see Bob Brand, Larry Kerr's acting boss.

Day 22.

Wednesday. At 8:45am I walked to the embassy to see Bob Brand. Jorge met me at the lobby and took me to Bob Brand's office. Brand said, "Washington told them to back off the case." He didn't explain the statement. I went away shocked, and disappointed. Maybe not disappointed but disillusioned.

I immediately called Leo Crampsey at work in Wilmington, Delaware. He said, "Don't worry about it, I will call Washington now."

Apparently, Leo did some good. Larry Kerr, late that day called me, which was unusual, and said, "The embassy will assist me as soon as the court order is issued." What a relief!

He also said that he didn't think it was proper for me to expedite the court order to the Chief of Police in Mixco. He said he would talk to Judge Calderon (this is the first time I heard the judge's name). Larry would contact the police—I thought to myself, this will take another week. These statements confused me. I didn't know I was going to expedite the court order to the police in the first place, unless this was a deal Maria and the judge made. I had no reason to believe the embassy was going to be involved.

I talked with Maria and she requested I come to her office and bring my passport. I hailed a taxi and was on my way. I signed some sort of application in her presence and she made a copy of my passport. She said, "Everything will be turned over to the judge today." I was surprised: I thought the judge had everything a couple days ago. "Maybe the court order will be issued <u>tomorrow</u>," she said.

I went shopping and bought gifts for Mary Ann, Jen, Debbie and a shirt for Jimmy. The Roy Nelsons bought clothes for Jimmy, pants, shirt, belt, shorts, shoes and socks. This was very considerate of them.

I had written a letter to Maureen and Bob telling them my feelings on their kidnapping. I was going to give the letter to them once I had Jimmy. The Nelsons read the letter.

I called Leo Crampsey that evening and asked him if he could get Jorge to help me through these, hopefully final days. My major concern was not being able to communicate with the police. I had great faith in Jorge and very little in the rest of the embassy. I was particularly disturbed by Bob Brand's comments. Leo said he would call Washington tomorrow and request Jorge be used to help.

Day 23.

Thursday April 17, 1986—Another tomorrow . . .

Up at 2:00am, never went back to sleep.

All morning I tried calling Maria. First, the phone line was dead, then it was busy. The phone system in Guatemala was very bad. Sometimes it took hours getting through. I called her office several times and her secretary told me she would not be in until tomorrow.

Finally, late afternoon I got Maria at home. She said, "I just left the judge. He is still reviewing the papers and may have the court order ready tomorrow, if not, Monday." My notes said, "Must have faith and patience—but God it's hard."

"I don't know how many more tomorrows I can stand," I said in my notes.

I talked to Jorge two more times that day. The first time he said, he and the Consulate at the embassy (I don't know who this was), went to Mixco and saw the Chief of Police, who was to pick up Jimmy. Jorge and the Chief of Police were good friends: they would cooperate as soon as the court order was issued. I wondered if Leo's call to Washington inspired this or Larry Kerr's good sense.

The second time Jorge said, in his normal optimistic view, if the court order is issued tomorrow, Jimmy can be picked up in the evening and we can leave on Saturday. Bob and Maureen will be arrested if they resist.

I talked to Larry Kerr in the afternoon, his tone was very pleasant.

Mary Ann said, Leo called her and said every thing was straightened out in Washington. This explains the Embassy's turn around. Mary Ann said everyone will be disappointed if Jimmy and I don't get home this weekend.

DAY 24.

Friday. The day God made and the Devil took away.

This day started with much hope and ended in total despair. The hope was the judge would issue the court order today, the despair was it didn't happen.

During the day, I talked with Larry and Maria a couple of times.

I was interested if Larry had talked to Judge Calderon. He said, "No," however, he mentioned the American Consulate, Dorothy Trujillo, along with Bob Brand, was talking to the judge as we spoke. He said he would call me back and let me know what transpired.

Late that afternoon, I contacted Maria at home. She said, "The Judge would have the court order Monday!" I wrote in my notes, "I don't believe her." She said, "She saw the judge at 1:30pm and the American Consulate had talked to him."

After many tries, I reached Larry Kerr at home that evening. He said he was not on the case and didn't know what transpired. I reminded him, that morning, he said he would call me back. This must have annoyed him because he said to me in a stern tone, "The Libyan situation is more important than a family problem." That crushed me. I agree the Libyan situation is important but he promised to call me and he didn't and this didn't show much character.

Larry recommended I call Bob Brand for information, but wouldn't give me his home phone number; he said, call the embassy, which was closed.

Larry also said to me, hiring a lawyer was the wrong thing to do, I should have gone to the judge myself. This was the most ridiculous statement I heard the whole time in Guatemala and contradicts what he told me previously. Without a lawyer, I would never have rescued Jimmy legally and I couldn't even speak to the judge because of the language barrier.

Larry did offer to go with me to see Judge Calderon on Monday at 8:00am, this made me feel a lot better.

I called Bob Brand that evening and left a message for him to call me. Apparently he checked his calls because he called me from his home. I asked him what transpired with the judge, he said, "He wasn't sure, maybe Dorothy Trujillo would know." I almost flipped. Was he there?

In order to contact Dorothy, I called the security guard at the embassy, because the embassy was closed. He said he would call her at home and leave a message that I wanted to speak with her and it was urgent.

About an hour later, she returned my call. I introduced myself. This was the first time I spoke with her. I asked her what transpired with Judge Calderon. She said, the judge told her he just received the papers that day, Friday. This is unbelievable. Someone is lying. Could it be the Judge? She was to call the judge by 3:00pm on Monday to get his input. I just cannot put into words how exasperated I felt.

I had a long chat with Dorothy. I strongly expressed my feelings to her. She said to me, Mr. Kuty, do you play golf? I said, "Yes." She then asked, "Would you like to go golfing with me tomorrow?" After a little thought, I said, "Yes."

I needed some outlet, I thought golfing would help. I was wondering if I weren't the prisoner, not Bob.

Mary Ann was very disappointed when I talked with her that night. She had told every one that I would be home that weekend. Debbie was at our house and I talked with her. She was devastated. Both Debbie and Mary Ann cried.

Day 25 and 26.

Saturday and Sunday

Dorothy Trujillo picked me up in her diesel Rabbit Volkswagen at 8:30am, to go golfing. Had a pleasant day golfing. Had a 106, which was pretty bad. After golfing we chatted. Dorothy was very noncommittal. She made no promises to help, but she would pray. She said, "Jerry Wilson would like for me to visit him at his house on Sunday." Is this a change in the embassy's attitude?

I contacted Larry Kerr on Sunday and asked if his offer to see Judge Calderon on Monday was still on the table. He said, "Yes and I was to meet him at the embassy at 9:00am."

Had lunch with the Roy Nelsons and thirty missionaries.

I waited to 7:00pm to hear from Jerry Wilson about his invite to his house. I called him. He apologized, he said he and his wife were ill and weren't up to it. One would think he could have called.

CHAPTER 13
PART IV

Days 27 and 28

The Court Order and More Setbacks

DAY 27.

Monday, April 21 1986. Arrived at the embassy at 9:00am. Larry Kerr said he talked to Dorothy Trujillo and learned that she was to call the judge at 12:00 noon and he would give her a decision. I explained that my understanding from her was, she was to call at 3:00pm for information and it was not clear that a decision had not already been made. (I was trying to put pressure on Larry for us to see the Judge as soon as possible). Also, she thought it was a good idea for you and me to see the judge. Larry agreed to call the Judge that morning and I would wait in the lobby to hear the judge's decision.

At 10:00 o'clock Larry came to the lobby and said, "We will leave in 5 minutes."

Larry and I along with two security guards carrying shotguns, got in a bulletproof sedan, went to the Court House in Guatemala City.

We met Judge Calderon, a 65 year old, round, short, balding Guatemalan. Larry started to plead my case in Spanish and the judge burst out in laughter. I was perplexed. What was so funny! Judge Calderon handed Larry the Court Order! He said, he expected the order to be carried out that day or the next (It never happened). Judge

Calderon's secretary recorded it and we were on our way. I WAS OVERJOYED, (but the mission wasn't over).

As Larry and I were leaving the Court House we met Bob Brand and Jorge Lemus on the Court House steps. We told them we had the court order. Jorge asked to see and read it. It was in Spanish. He said the court order, in addition to directing the police to pick up Jimmy and Bob having to turn Jimmy over to me, that a member of the U.S. Embassy was to accompany me.

Jorge suggested we meet at the embassy at 1:30 in the afternoon to determine the next plan of action. The guards dropped Larry off at the embassy. Larry asked to keep the Court Order to make copies. ***This was the biggest mistake I made on the whole trip.*** I was expecting the plan of action would include taking the court order to the Chief of Police in Mixco today and tomorrow have Jimmy picked up. Well it didn't happen.

The guards dropped me off at the hotel.

I called Maria about getting the court order. She already knew about it. We were both very happy. She was to meet me at the hotel to settle our account at 8:00 tonight. This never happened because of the following events.

After 1:30 in the afternoon came and went and no one called me about the get together. I started calling. I tried Jorge and Larry Kerr but couldn't get through to them. The first one I could get was Bob Brand. He informed me that Larry Kerr was handling the get together and would meet with the police. He said, "Larry will call you back." I asked Brand if Washington called last week and he said, "Yes." I asked him, "what did they say." He said, "to cooperate".

By the time Larry called later in the afternoon, the idea to deliver the court order to the Mixco Police was not possible—too late. Then he said to me, "Your lawyer should deliver the court order to the Chief of Police." When he told me that, I exploded. I asked him, "What happened to the 1:30pm get together you were to arrange?" His reply was, "After thinking about it, the handling of the arrangements is your lawyer's duty." I said, "Why on Gods earth didn't you call me so I could of arranged something." "You are holding the court order and you are holding me hostage."

Now the bastard is backing out. Another day or more is wasted.

That afternoon I contacted Maria at home. I told her what Larry Kerr had said. This upset her, she remarked, "The embassy always backs out." In order to issue the court order, she needed to know what the police had been told as well as the original court order. I told her Larry Kerr has the original but I will get it.

I called Larry Kerr at the embassy and said, I needed the original Court Order immediately. I also gave him another piece of my mind. He said he would send it over in twenty minutes. He sent it by messenger and I signed for it. Larry Kerr had been a thorn in my side. Sometimes he is very helpful, sometimes not. Sometimes he makes promises, then he breaks them. I just cannot figure him out. This trait doesn't get better.

Maria called me. She said Bob Brand called her. She asked me to come to her office with the court order. I took a taxi and met with her. She decided we should go to the Secretary General's Office in the police station in Guatemala City to get the court order recorded and signed. I really didn't know why. She commented, before the new government took over one would have to pay the Secretary General before he would sign it. When we got back to Maria's office she wanted to talk to Larry Kerr for advice. They talked in Spanish for fifteen minutes. Among other things, she told me Larry said, "The embassy doesn't want to get involved because they represent all Americans, and if he were a grandfather and was afraid of the boy getting hurt, (meaning me) he wouldn't pursue it." THANK YOU Mr. Kerr, I hope your grandson doesn't get kidnapped.

Maria drove me to the hotel. When I got in the car I rolled down the window and buckled my seat belt. She said, "You are a good American but not a good Guatemalan." Then she asked me to roll up the window and lock the door. She proceeded to tell me it was common for people to reach in the window or yank the door open and grab anything they could reach. She would contact me the first thing the next morning. I kept the court order.

Jorge and I talked. I asked him if he knew if the police in Bob's district had been alerted yet. He said not to his knowledge, but the Director General, whose last name was Zuccinni could speak English, was informed. Jorge said Zuccinni was out of town. A Martinez Hermanis, who was a friend of Jorge, was the acting Chief of Police in Bob's district. Jorge said he would check things out and will call me back.

Made my usual calls to bring everyone up to speed. Mary Ann was elated to hear I finally got the court order.

The next call from Jorge changed all the plans. Jorge took control!

At 9:15pm Jorge called, He said he met with the Chief of Police, Martinez Hermanis, in Bob's area in Mixco. He explained in detail the situation and informed Martinez that Bob had Doberman security dogs, may be armed, and might resist. They laid out a plan to either pick up Bob and Jimmy tomorrow evening, or the next morning while they were asleep. Martinez wanted me and an interpreter to come to the police station the next morning with the court order.

During the night I decided to see if Cecil Nelson would help me deliver the court order to the Mixco police.

I didn't sleep much that night.

DAY 28.

Tuesday, Progress.

At 6:15am, I'm sitting on the edge of the bed, somewhat in a vacuum. Trying to coordinate this activity was a challenge, especially when I couldn't speak Spanish.

At 8:00am I called Cecil Nelson and asked him if he would go with me to Mixco and make arrangements with the Chief of Police, Martinez Hermanis. He said he would, and added he knew Chief Hermanis. He would pick me up within the hour. He offered to put the house under surveillance.

While waiting I called Maria. I informed her I would not need her that day. I think she felt relieved because she wanted to talk. She said, "She spent three days with Judge Calderon trying to convince him the embassy would assist. He did not trust the embassy because they always back out and leave it up to someone else." When Larry Kerr said, she should deliver the court order to the police, she said, "This is what Calderon was afraid of."

I told her it seems you have to die sometimes before you can live. Friday was my day of death because I couldn't find out anything. She said, "Friday was my day to live because she knew the judge agreed to issuing the court order."

Cecil Nelson picked me up at 9:15am and we traveled approximately eight miles to the police station in Mixco. Cecil gave the court order to the Chief and briefly went over the pick-up plan. The Chief said they decided to do the pick-up the next morning at 6:00am.

Cecil brought me back to the hotel. I made a zillion phone calls.

Maria came over to the hotel and I paid her $2,500 for her services. She offered her house if it would aid in getting Jimmy home. Neither she nor I realized that I would need her again.

I called the embassy and could only get Dorothy Trujillo. I told her what was happening. I mentioned, should the Mixco police pick up Jimmy at 6:00am, I planned to catch a plane at 7:00am to Costa Rica. As we were talking Larry Kerr came into her office. He got on the phone and said, "Mr. Kuty your plan stinks,"(*that's nice Larry*) "because you can't make a 7:00 o'clock flight." (*you're probably right Larry, so I'll make a later flight*). Besides immigration won't let Jimmy go because they want to photograph him and take his finger prints. (*Thanks Larry for telling me at the last minute what needs to be done*).

I didn't know who was going to do what, I'd just play it by ear.

Cecil Nelson called and said Jimmy was seen yesterday and today riding his bicycle.

I called Jerry Wilson at the embassy and again asked for Jorge's help. Once again, he refused. Jorge was already helping me but I was hoping Jerry and the other embassy members would soften during these final days and hours.

Jorge called late that evening. He told me Jerry Wilson stopped in his office that afternoon and told him, "To get the hell off the case."

I was concerned as to how I was going to communicate with the police in the morning after they picked up Jimmy. I asked Jorge if he would arrange to have the police contact him and he in turn would call me. He agreed.

I thanked Jorge for everything he did to help me. I told him I was sorry Jerry Wilson was so spiteful to reprimand him. Jorge kept saying, "No problem, no problem."

I had put out a $500 reward for information leading to Jimmy's whereabouts when Jorge first discovered they entered Guatemala. The Embassy was holding it. I told Jorge it was his. **Jorge you're a hero**.

I called Mary Ann and said the police plan to pick up Jimmy at six o'clock the next morning.

It's in God's hands. I am whipped.

CHAPTER 13
PART V

Days 29 and 30

Getting Jimmy—Wasn't Easy

DAY 29.

Wednesday, April 23, 1986. Woke up at 4:30am. I had a lot on my mind. How was I going to get from the hotel to the police station? Was the embassy going to assist me with Jimmy and help get him a passport? I was undecided whether to fly to Costa Rica or to take Eastern to Miami. The Eastern Manager had guaranteed seats at any time. How was Jimmy going to react? Andy Rodgers had his physician prescribe Valium, for Jimmy, if needed, which I had in my possession.

This was it, the big day. This was the morning the police were to pick up Jimmy at 6:00am.

Had trouble getting in touch with Jorge or Maria to find out what was happening. The tension was mounting.

At 7:20am Jorge called and said, "They have Jimmy and go to the police station as soon as possible!"

I was beginning to panic because I needed an interpreter. I couldn't get through to Maria. I called the Roy Nelsons. Ethyl, Roy's wife answered. I asked if they could go to the police in Mixco and help as an interpreter. Ethyl said Roy was sick with a fever but would see what could be done.

I knew I couldn't call Jorge because Jerry Wilson would have him fired.

At the last minute, I got through to Maria. I asked her if she could go to the Mixco Police station. She said she would but it would take about forty five minutes.

I went to the lobby to get a taxi. Hardly anyone was there and no one could speak English. A bell boy, who could speak some English, came to my aid, got me a taxi and gave the police address to the taxi driver.

The problem was the driver and I could not communicate and the driver got lost twice on the way. He had to stop a policeman to get directions.

What tension.

Finally, I got there.

Paid the taxi driver and asked him to stay a bit. I was thinking I would go in, pick up Jimmy and go back to the hotel. It didn't happen that way.

I walked into the police station, on April 23, 1986, my twenty-ninth day in Guatemala, and there sat a startled Bob Freels.

"What in the hell are you doing here?" Freels asked.

"I came to take my grandson home." I replied.

I went to the Chief of Police's office. Freels followed as well as Freel's neighbor, who came with him and could speak some English. Freels wanted to know what was going on.

I tried to tell the Chief of Police to wait because my lawyer was coming. The neighbor got the Police Chief to finally understand.

I then learned, the Police picked up Bob <u>but did not pick up Jimmy or Maureen</u>!

I became panic stricken.

Oh my God, are we going to lose Jimmy? Now, it was a wait for my lawyer.

The Roy Nelsons arrived but I excused them because of the legal circumstances and when they saw Bob they became frightened.

While waiting, Freels insisted he make a phone call. I kept saying, "No phone calls, no phone calls." I knew his intent was to call Maureen and she and Jimmy would run. The police didn't understand me, but it made no difference anyway. In Guatemala, as in the United States, the accused has the right to make one call. He made his call. The police were getting nervous.

As the wait for the lawyer went on, Freels kept asking me questions. "Did the divorce go through?" I told him get a lawyer and find out. "Where are you staying?" I laughed and said "Are you kidding." He asked, "If I had a reward out for Jimmy," I replied that I was willing to pay for information. He mentioned people in Puerto Barrios knew of a reward.

I told him, "You got a lot of mercenary friends out there after your hide." It wasn't true, but I wanted to throw the fear of God into him. He asked, "Which mercenary informed on him." I just laughed.

I gave Bob a copy of the letter I wrote to him and Maureen. A copy is attached later.

Twenty minutes after I got to the police station, Maria, my lawyer arrived.

She took over.

She now learned Jimmy wasn't there.

Bob wanted to be released, but the police told him they had a court order and could hold him for twenty four hours.

Maria insisted the police get Jimmy immediately. Maria, the Chief of Police, two policemen, and I squeezed into her tiny Volkswagen and followed the neighbor of Freels through the crowded city to the suburbs for about 3 miles. Bob was detained at the police station.

The neighbor drove so fast, Maria could not keep up with him.

I requested that Maria ask the Chief of Police if they left a policeman to guard the house. He said, "No."

My heart sank, again.

We finally arrived, the neighbor and his wife were in the front of Freels' house. They said, "Maureen and the boy were not there." The Chief of Police told them if they didn't cooperate they would be arrested. After some coercing, Maureen came out of a nearby house. When asked, where was Jimmy, at first she said, Little Jimmy was at school. When the police said they would go get him, she admitted he was not at school. Maureen then revealed he was at a friend's house about five blocks away. Maria, the Police Chief, two policemen and a neighbor drove there and, sure enough, Jimmy was there with his suitcase packed. They returned him to his house.

When Jimmy saw me, his grandfather, tears trickled down his freckled face, put his suitcase down and came and hugged me. Guess what I did? I cried.

He didn't do or say much of anything. It was a crushing, emotional scene. Everyone shed tears, including Maureen, Maria, the neighbors and even the police. I now knew I did the right thing.

When things settled a bit, I had a chance to talk with Maureen. I asked her if I could take pictures. She invited me into the house to take pictures of the dogs, for Jimmy's keepsake. She said she was having problems with Bob's lying and telling stories. She said he is paranoid. I let her read the letter I wrote to both of them.

Maureen with Dogs

The letter to Bob Freels and Maureen Wilkin.

4/5/1986

Bob and Maureen,

By now you know we have Jimmy safely home.

I'm sorry you choose to devastate several families for your own selfish end. I hope you learned that you can not violate society's laws and never be found. Remember, when you deal with devious people, and some mercenaries are devious people, you're never free.

I know how you both feel because we went through the same emotions. Feels like your heart has been ruptured. After you have a chance to think this through, you will realize you went about it in the wrong way. What you have done violates society's and nature's laws.

Maureen, your mother and Bevin are devastated. I understand your mother has been hospitalized twice with heart problems since you left. You owe her a call to insure her you still care. I also understand Bevin can't understand why she cannot see you.

Maureen, you are not Jimmy's mother, you are Bevin's mother. Diane can provide for Bevin but she cannot be her mother. You could and should be Bevin's mother.

Maureen, if you work with society, within its laws, you still can have a good life and share your loved ones. Although you choose to cheat society and your friends you haven't done anything serious except your involvement in this abduction. You can clear your monetary problems easily. If you choose to work out the past, I would not prosecute.

Bob, your problems with devious people exceed your problems of sharing Jimmy. I don't know how you'll ever mend your problems of lying, cheating, exaggerating, and misleading your supposed friends.

I'm impressed with your new life. It could be a good one for Jimmy if it were done under the proper circumstances. Jimmy should not be raised having to be watched, in hiding and protected like you're doing. He should not be living under the shroud of mercenaries being involved. Both of you should realize you are violating Jimmy's rights, and Bevin's, to share the love of both parents. This is immoral and illegal. Bob, it appears the illegal aspect doesn't bother you, but it should, because where ever you are, or go, you will be faced with it. If you are a moral human being, you have to realize Jimmy has the right to share his parents. You should not take that away from him. Although you have broken the laws of two countries, we realize Jimmy's rights and needs to share both parents is paramount. Maybe Jimmy's rights can be granted if you go about it rationally. It is up to you.

JIM KUTY

I mentioned to Maureen to call her mother. She didn't comment but asked me to call her when I get back. I thought this was cold.

I told her I realize Jimmy should be shared by both parents, and if he co-operated, arrangements could be made for him to see Jimmy.

I requested Jimmy's passport. Maureen said they were all at someone else's house. On the way back to the police station, Maureen and Jimmy rode with me, Maria, and the Police Chief. We stopped at this "someone else's house," but no one was home. Two other vehicles, containing some neighbors, accompanied us to the Mixco police station.

At the police station, the Police Chief started to read the court order, that was in Spanish, giving me custody of my grandson. When he got to the part that said, "The U.S. Embassy had to be present," he stopped and said something in Spanish. Maria turned to me and said, "Where is the embassy member?" "They're not here," I replied. **"The chief said he cannot turn the boy over to you unless a member of the embassy is here," Maria said.**

The drama wasn't over yet.

There are no words that can express my feelings at that moment: anger, helplessness, devastation, and frustration are a few.

"Damn it," I said. "Give me the phone." I knew the Embassy's number by heart because I called them every day. I got Larry Kerr.

"Are you going to come out here and help me? You know what the court order said. Are you going to send anybody?" I asked Larry.

Larry said, **"No."**

"Here's my lawyer, talk to her."

Maria got on the phone and talked to Larry for fifteen minutes in Spanish.

"What's the verdict?" I asked.

I've been authorized to represent the U.S. Embassy," she said.

She turned to the Chief of Police and told him in Spanish that she was authorized to represent the U.S. Embassy, He bought it. I got the boy.

IT WAS ALL OVER!

The finishing touches were for Bob to sign documents turning Jimmy over to me.

Bob asked, what could he do legally to prevent Jimmy from leaving? Maria told him he could do nothing. His only recourse was to start legal proceedings in the states.

Finally, we both signed the record.

The parting of Bob Freels and his son was an emotional one.

Bob hugged Jimmy, slipped an antique silver dollar into his hands and sobbed. So did Maureen and Jimmy.

Even the neighbors who had come to say goodbye to the American boy had tears in their eyes.

"Don't forget, Jimmy, come back and see us," they sighed.

It was shortly after 12:30pm.

After the way things finally worked out, I no longer felt our lives were in danger. I saw no need to try and rush out of Guatemala. I decided to stay over night and leave in the morning. I decided to have a party that night at five o'clock in my hotel room.

There were some things yet to do.

Maria, Jimmy and I drove to the embassy in Maria's car to get Jimmy a passport. To our surprise, Larry Kerr had a soda and sandwich already prepared for Jimmy. Even with this act of kindness Larry Kerr would not get involved with the passport.

I called Andy Rodgers. His comment was "Damn the embassy." Andy said, "He knew the head of immigration," who was the brother of President Marco Vinicio. Andy said, "You go to immigration and everything will be arranged." Arranged it was.

Maria, Jimmy and I went to immigration. They immediately took his picture, finger printed him, and gave us a passport so Jimmy could get on the airplane.

See, Andy Rodgers was influential again.

Maria brought me to the hotel and the three of us ate a late lunch.

We then went to visit Andy. He was elated. He and Maria talked in Spanish for a long time.

I said my goodbyes to Maria and we parted. What a gal!

I started my calling to inform everyone and invited them to the party. Called: 1)Susan Rodgers, she already knew we had Jimmy, she almost screamed over the phone. She said she was making the airplane arrangement and would bring the tickets to the party; 2)Jorge Lemus; 3)Cecil Nelson; 4)Roy and Ethyl Nelson and the embassy staff. Everyone came except the embassy staff.

Andy Rodgers assigned a security guard full time to Jimmy and me.

Jimmy and I took a dip in the hotel pool.

I called Bill Cregar and Leo Crampsey at work in Wilmington, Delaware. I never heard a happier man than Leo Crampsey. What a new friend.

Jimmy talked to his mom, Debbie, MaryAnn and my other daughter, Jennifer. I gave them our flight information.

On retiring for the night, Jimmy said to me, **"When he was 21 he was coming home."** {meaning to his mother}.

DAY 30.

Thursday, April 24, 1986. The best night's rest I had in 30 days.

Andy Rodgers took Jimmy and me to the airport in the hotel's private car. He, along with the Eastern airline manager, walked us through customs and saw us boarding the plane to Philadelphia via Miami.

The reunion turned out to be a chaotic affair.

The plane was two hours late. The airport waiting room was a mass of relatives toting, "Welcome Home" balloons, anxious travelers wondering what was going on, reporters and photographers who had gotten word of Jimmy's arrival.

I was emotionally drained. "If you were to say boo to me, I would have cried."

For a tired, somewhat confused nine year old, it was a bit frightening.

Spotting his mother through the crowd, Jimmy ran to her. Debbie pulled Jimmy to her chest and hugged him tightly.

"I was elated," she recalls, "I was so happy to have him home."

Ron Devlin, of the MORNING CALL newspaper of Allentown, Pennsylvania, said, "Kuty had taken thirty days of vacation and in thirty days he had done the impossible."

Leo Crampsey told a reporter, "Frankly, I wouldn't have given a plug nickel for the chances of locating that boy in Guatemala." "The tenacity of Jim Kuty's endeavors was amazing."

"30 days of Hell," I was glad it was over.

Jimmy Debbie Dawn

Afterward

James Robert (Jimmy) Freels, III—My grandson, is now thirty six years old (2013). He is married, his wife's name is Cheryl, and has two children. Their names are Jimmy Freels, IV, age sixteen and a daughter, Jessica, age ten. Jimmy works as a foreman installing natural gas pipelines in the construction industry. He is also in real estate and owns thirteen rentals. For some reason he likes to hunt and ski, like me.

He lives ten miles from us and our family life is very close.

James Robert (Bob) Freels, Jr—Jimmy's father, separated from Maureen about a month after Jimmy came home. A couple months after that, he moved back to the states. He remarried and is now living in Alabama. He occasionally communicates with his son.

Maureen came back to live with her mother but migrated to Florida. As far as I know, she resides there now.

About the Author

I was born on January 8, 1932, in Dutch Hill, Pennsylvania. Dutch Hill is located on a steep slope between LaBelle, PA., at the top of the hill, and at the bottom a small coal mining community of Maxwell. It is located about thirty five miles south of Pittsburgh, PA., and borders the Monongahela River.

I grew up, played, and went to grade and high school together with about a dozen friends on Dutch Hill. We were poor but happy kids, never realizing what hardships our parents endured during the depression.

My grandfather, Paul Kuty, was killed in a mine cave-in at age forty five, leaving grandma with nine children. Mom, dad and my sister, Irene, who was 6 years older than I, lived with my grandmother and two of her children, Irma and Jimmy Kuty. The rest were grown and scattered.

We had no running water. The water was supplied by an outside pump and carried inside with buckets. The toilet was an outhouse— cold in the winter. There was no central heat. Heating the house and water was done by a coal stove in the kitchen.

In grade school, I was a tinkerer. I built model airplanes, developed my photos from my Brownie box camera and learned taxidermy. At this early age my philosophy was, "If someone could do something, I could do it too," and I did.

High school was in Brownsville, PA. six school bus miles away. As a freshman, I came down with rheumatic fever. The coal mine superintendent's daughter, Virginia Beerbower, a neighbor, brought my homework to me. This enabled me to be promoted to tenth grade. I made good grades in high school. Upon graduation in 1949, I was awarded the prodigious "Bausch and Lomb Science" trophy.

On graduation, I had no idea what I was going to do. It seemed my only alternative was to join the military service. <u>Then the most important thing in my life occurred.</u> My sixth grade teacher, Frank Trun, a neighbor, visited our family and said he thought he could get me a college scholarship based on my grades, as well as, being a hardship case. He did, which led me to going to the University of Pittsburgh majoring in chemical engineering in 1949.

In order to live near campus and go to school I needed to work. I worked at the University's cafeteria for my meals and part-time at the Carnegie Mellon Institute for my living expenses. On weekends and during the summer of 1950, in my freshman year of college, my mom and I built a new home for mom and dad. If that wasn't enough, I was introduced to my future wife, Mary Ann Friend, by my college buddy, Francis Asti. Going to school, working, building a house, and courting about did me in.

In 1952, I got married. Now I had to get a full time job and went to work for Pittsburgh Coke and Chemical on Neville Island outside Pittsburgh while going to school. Mary Ann helped by working. We had our first daughter, Jennifer, in 1952 and our second daughter, Debbie, in 1954. I graduated in 1954. At graduation, I was honored with "The Outstanding Engineering and Mines Student Award." My parents were very proud of me.

I went to work for Du Pont in 1954 at their Chemical Plant in Deepwater, New Jersey across the Delaware River from their corporate headquarters in Wilmington, Delaware, called the "Chambers Works." I continued to work for Du Pont until I retired in 1989.

In 1956, I built the house I still live in today, in Woodstown, New Jersey. It took me nine months of working nights and weekends with the help of family and friends to complete.

It was in 1985 and 1986, I searched and rescued my grandson from Guatemala.

One of my goals was to become a millionaire. I did that too. Part of that objective was not to become wealthier. I retired at 58 years old and enjoyed my good fortune with my family, friends, and those in need.

I accomplished a great deal during those working and retirement years.

In 1970, at the age of 38, Mary Ann and I learned to ski. Starting in 1971, we skied Aspen, CO. for seventeen consecutive years. We skied several places in Europe and Canada, and all over the United States. At 81 years old (2013), we still ski. It is a family sport and our children, grandchildren, and great grandchildren go with us.

I've always hunted and have hunted all over the North American continent. Today my den is full of trophies that I mounted.

Did a little golfing too. Once had a 71.

At the age of 68, one of my two daughters, Jennifer, asked me to build her a log house. It took me two years to do it. It was featured in the October 2002 edition of the "Log Home Living" magazine.

I got into real estate. Bought some apartments and repaired them myself. They were and are still profitable. Purchased a couple houses in Houston, Texas, in the mid 1980's when the economy collapsed due to an oil crisis. In the turn around, I made a nice profit.

I was always thrifty, progressive and hard working (I think) at the same time. I was the first person in our township to install solar panels, much of which I did myself. Haven't had an electric bill in two years. I drive a Toyota Prius C hybrid and get 50—60 miles per gallon of gasoline.

All these things helped me to attain my financial goals and make for a comfortable, happy life. As I mentioned before, "If someone else could do it, I could do it too." This attitude and perseverance that I inherited from my parents, helped me find Jimmy.